The Politics of Scholarly Gentlemen

Brahman-Maratha Conflict in an Indian University 1924 - 1995

Dr. Donald V. Kurtz
Professor Emeritus, University of Wisconsin - Milwaukee
Adjunct Faculty, University of Texas - San Antonio

India Research Press
New Delhi

India Research Press
Flat-6, Khan Market, New Delhi – 110 003.
Ph.: 24694610, 24694855; Telefax : 24618637, 41757113
bahrisons@vsnl.com; contact@indiaresearchpress.com
www.indiaresearchpress.com

2009

ISBN thirteen: 978-81-8386-036-2
ISBN ten: 81-8386-036-9

Dr. Donald V. Kurtz
The Politics of Scholarly Gentlemen

Cataloguing in Publication Data
1. Education 2. University Politics 3. South Asia
4. Brahman 5. Maratha 6. Pune, India

I. Title II. Author

Printed for *India Research Press* at Focus Impressions, New Delhi-110 003

Preface

Most people, even the scholars who work in them, do not know much about the culture and politics of universities. Certainly their pedagogic and educational functions are important. But to insiders – teachers and administrators – they often are subordinate to other university functions, such as scholarly research and management of the institution, each of which can be fraught with conflict and competition. As modern institutions, universities are rarely thought to be exotic places. Such depictions are left to writers of fiction (see Smiley 1995; Haynes 2002), and these, as compared to scholarly studies, often depict the world of academia as more exotic than most people would think. In anthropology the study of universities has not received much attention largely because they do not seem to comply with the commitment of many anthropologists to the study of cultures in more exotic, esoteric, and erotic settings. I believe, however, that a deep examination of the culture and organisation of universities would reveal them to be as exotic, erotic, and esoteric as any "primitive society". (How many people, for example, would think of universities as game reserves in which female stüdents provide the quarry, frequently all too easily captured, for scholarly gentlemen acting out their primordial predisposition as hunters?) And when it comes to politics, the use of power by political agents to pursue public (and private) goals, the practices of scholarly gentlemen can be remarkably vicious.

From a less exotic perspective, how many people would think of the politics of a university as a microcosm of the politics that transpire in the national and international arenas with which we are more familiar? Politics in these arenas often involve fights among leaders over access to power that will allow them to control state governments and government agencies. Universities are rarely thought of as arenas that reflect similar processes. After all, is education not the primary business of universities? Yet, at Poona University,[1] in the state of Maharashtra in western India, the focus of this study, the politics in which the university's political leaders engaged historically, for the last 80 years, was precisely aimed at control of university government. And the strategies and tactics these leaders brought to the politics to control its government were as creative and novel as any we find in other, more commonly known political arenas. The point is, universities provide at least the same array of potential domains for socio-cultural analysis as any setting in which anthropologists conduct research.

There are many advantages to conducting anthropological research in universities. They are available. They are open to study, by and large. Research within them of an applied, ethnographic, theoretical, interpretive, symbolic – whatever the orientation or paradigm – is limited only by one's scholarly orientation. Any epistemology or paradigmatic framework is amenable to their socio-cultural contents. And professors, like politicians, are marvellous informants. They share a self-indulgent sciolism which, as with politicians, fosters a predilection to inform others about what they know, which they think is everything – as well as what they do not know, which is likely to be a lot. When this penchant for talk is conjoined in one status – professors cum politicians – as it was at Poona University, a rich and natural research environment emerges.

The Data

I gathered the data for this study over several years. In 1980-

1981, I spent five weeks on the postgraduate campus of Poona University. I was ancillary to a project to study litigation in Indian Universities. My real interest was in the politics of education. The visit to Poona opened the door for me to explore that interest in an Indian university.

The university's Anthropology Department invited me to return in 1983 as a University Grants Commission (UGC) Visiting Professor of Anthropology.[2] During the five months I spent at the campus. I used the grant of Rs 1,000—the UGC award provided to develop and circulate a questionnaire that elicited general and specific information about the university. About 144 teachers, about 50 per cent at that time, responded. Over 60 indicated a willingness to be interviewed in more detail and I did this with 43 before I left. Many became invaluable informants later. The data provided background information on the university, the society and culture of its personnel, and information on their politics.

In 1985-1986 I spent nine months at the postgraduate campus as a senior Fulbright scholar. It was during this period that I gathered most of what constitutes the ethnographic present for this work. Most of the research was conducted on the postgraduate campus, the nerve centre of Poona University. But I also visited and interviewed the staffs of colleges that were important to the university's politics. In summer of 1989, I returned for a month to catch up on events after 1986. This data provides the material for Chapter 9. In 1994-1995 I spent five months at the university and in 2002 another month to conclude the research. The data from 2002 provides the basis for Chapter 10 and updated information that I insert in context throughout the work.

Informants

I interviewed about 80 individuals for this research, almost all of whom were involved in or knowledgeable of the specifics of the politics of Poona University. I conducted the interviews in English, the language of higher education in India.

One of the hallmarks of the critique of ethnography that emerged in the mid 1980s emphasized giving authoritative voice to one's informants – the "others" – and, correspondingly, muting that of the anthropologist. In this work I mute the voices of my informants and remain the anthropological authority. There are reasons for this. Almost all the subjects of this research are alive. Any voice given to them would be open to multiple interpretations and could leave them vulnerable to litigation by others who have political grudges to settle. Because of this I use anonyms for the individuals to whom I refer.

Nonetheless, I want to thank everyone who contributed to this project. I cannot mention all of them by name – there are too many – but I do want to acknowledge by name those who contributed most to this research (see endnote)[3]. Now that the university's politicians with whom I worked have been superseded by a younger generation and the conditions in which this research took place have changed, there is no reason not to.

Elsewhere, Professor Aswine Ray of Jawaharlal Nehru University, Professor Subha Reddy of Madras University, and Professor B. S. Baviskar of Delhi University provided me insights based upon their rich experiences in Indian higher education. The late Professor A. B. Shah, a "social worker", in Pune, helped in 1981 to steer me toward a study of Indian higher education, although I suspect my vision of the study differs from his. Paul Axelrod, Joe Di Bona, Karen Fustes, Jerry Hanson, Jim McDonald, Bill Merrill and Shirley White read all or parts of this work and made suggestions, many of which I followed. Ellen Ghere constructed Figures 1 and 2. Jean Mitchell proofread the manuscript. Again, I extend my thanks to each of them.

Plan of the Book

First, I have a comment on the Appendix. There are many dimensions to the university's politics. The six episodes that comprise the Appendix are designed to provide the reader insight into the conflicts that these politics evoked. Each episode is a case study of the conflict induced by the politics of the university's leader and political agents. The episodes do not relate directly to the politics involved in the fights to control university government. Instead they are the fallout of those fights. They show on the one hand how the leader's politics affected the lives and careers of particular leaders and agents and, on the other, how contradictions in the organization of the university evoked symbols and ideologies that were important to the university's history of political conflict. The episodes can be read at any time. But they will be more meaningful if they are read in some context. At the end of appropriate chapters I recommend episodes that will provide additional insight into the topics and events just covered. I also refer to these episodes at points in the text where they have some relevance. To become familiar with the political leaders and agents that are addressed in the episodes see the list of *dramatis personae* following the introduction (The leaders and their projects are considered in detail in Chapter 3).

The introduction to the book provides a glimpse of the politics of the university and explores the ideas that were important to make sense out of the data. Chapter 1 describes the postgraduate campus and the city and rural colleges that comprise Poona University. Chapter 2 sets the stage for the analysis that follows by presenting the background to the university's politics. Chapter 3 introduces the leaders of the political teams that were involved in the fights and their political projects. Chapters 4 through 7 analyse the conflict that involved the politics of these leaders. Chapter 4 traces the conflict from the first conceptualization of the university in 1924 to 1970. Chapter 5 spans the period from 1970 to 1978 during which the introduction of a new University Act in 1974[4] became the source of much subsequent political fighting. Chapter 6 explores how the political projects of some leaders dominated the university between 1974 and 1982. Chapter 7 takes the study to 1989 when new agents in the arena destroyed the political careers of some of these leaders. Chapter 8 analyses the politics that were internal and external to the university between 1989 and 1995. In 1995 the last leader with whom I was associated in this drama retired as Vice-Chancellor. An Epilogue and the Appendix conclude the work.

Notes

1. In February 1995, the university administration erased one more example of British etymological conceit and changed the name of the university from Poona University to Pune University. But, since all but the last two months of the research related to this project was conducted at Poona University I retain that name in the text. The British name for the city where the university is located, also Poona, was changed to Pune in the 1980s. In the text I refer to the city as Pune.
2. The University Grants Commission is the agency of the central government that oversees and coordinates the affairs of Indian universities and provides funds for higher education programs and development.

3. The structure, organization, and practice of the governments of Indian universities are established by University Acts. Statutes associated with these Acts codify the legal limits and powers of university governments. These Acts and their statutes are legislated by the governments of the states in which the universities are located and the senates of each university.

3. I extend my special and deepest thanks to each of the following for the selfless assistance they provided me in this research: S. K. Agarwala, M. R. Bhide, U. B. Bhoite, P. S. Bhosale, Narendra Bokhare, C. J. Daswani, D. N. Dhanagre, Ram Gambhir, S. C. Gupte, N. C. Joshi, S. B. Majumdar, Virendra N. Misra, Sohan P. Modak, R. K. Mutatkar, K. S. Nair, M. N. Palsane, S. Pandy, Nalini Paranjpe, P. N. Paranjpe, Shrikant Paranjpe, Bhushant Patwardan, N. S. Ramanama, S. P. Sathe, Gautan Sen, Nalinee Taralekar, S. N. Tawale, N. K. Thakare, Shirley White, Raju Vora.

Contents

Introduction

This ethnography is all about *politics*, raw, gut wrenching politics as it is practised by scholarly gentlemen who are not generally thought to be politicians. As noted earlier, politics is concerned with how leaders use power to attain public and private goals. The politics of Poona University is concerned with how historical *contradictions* embedded in the university provoked 70 years of strife and conflict between *leaders* who developed and used *political power* to acquire control of university *government*. The reason for these politics is simple. Whoever controlled university government controlled the university. Indeed, the politics of Poona University is a microcosm of the politics related to governments in general. But the politics of the university's agents is informative because it transpires in an unlikely place. Still, it would be helpful for the reader to know what I mean by the ideas involved in the university's politics and why they are important. (See Kurtz 2001 for a complete examination of the ideas that follow.)

I use a dialectical methodology to make sense of the university's politics. The essence of the dialectic as I use it argues that social systems, such as universities,comprised internal contradictions in social and cultural relations. Contradictions by their nature induce conflict between agents who represent the interests of the contradictory elements. The conflict in which they engage is aimed at resolving the contradiction in their favour. Since the idea of a contradiction is central to this work, it is worthwhile to consider it in more detail.

The idea of a contradiction refers to discrepancies, antagonisms, or oppositions in the relationship between entities within a social structure or institution, such as Poona University. The idea of a contradiction is important because attempts by human agents to resolve contradictory relations in a social system provide a major impetus for social and cultural change. However, contradictions that engender change exist only when certain conditions exist. First, a relationship must exist between two or more entities. Second, the entities must be constituted by virtue of being integral features of the structure. Third, the entities must be mutually interdependent. Finally the potential for conflict must exist by virtue of their relationship in the structure (Callinicos 1988:53). The contradictions in Poona University were embedded in relations of caste, institution and region.

In the traditional Hegelian and Marxist theories related to the ideas of the dialectic, conflict between opposed entities is resolved when one contradictory entity negates the existence of another. Today the idea of change as a result of the ongoing negation of opposing entities in social structures no longer has credibility. Instead, contradictory entities that are subordinated to others are not necessarily negated out of existence. They are more likely to become residual or remain dormant in the wings of those entities that have gained ascendancy in the social structure (Murphy 1971; Marquit, Moran, and Truit 1982; Kurtz 2001). As we shall see later, under certain conditions they may even regain their potential to challenge existing oppositions.

Conflict is the *modus operandi* of change induced by contradictory entities. Conflict induced by the attempts to resolve contradictions are distinctly a matter of politics when it evokes leaders who develop and use power to attain public and private goals. It need not be political or invested in political institutions. Conflict between contradictory entities can be embedded in other institutional contexts, such as economics, religion, even the family. But much of the conflict induced by contradictory relations does involve politics because, as in universities, it evokes leaders who use power to gain their ends.

As noted, the political conflict in Poona University was provoked by the existence of three multifaceted contradictions: caste, institution and region. My research suggested that the contradiction in caste relations – Brahmans, non-Brahmans (largely Marathas)[1] – was the primary cause of the history of conflict in the university. This contradiction emerged over 350 years ago in the region that is today the state of Maharashtra. About 80 years ago, when the university was first conceived, the contradiction in caste was complemented by others in the university's institutions – the postgraduate campus, city colleges, rural colleges – and the regional distribution of the colleges – urban and rural. These three contradictions in concert evoked politics and thrust leaders and their teams into conflict over control of the university's government, because – it's worth repeating – whoever was incumbent in the offices of university government thereby dominated and ran the university.

In these fights leaders of opposing teams developed and used material and ideological resources as political power to attain their goals (Kurtz 2001). Material resources refer primarily to those human agents who were allies of the leaders. Ideological resources derive from ideas and values inherent in caste identities and institutional affiliations. Brahmans affiliated with the city colleges believed that the colleges were superior pedagogically to the teachers and departments of the university's postgraduate campus. Teachers on the postgraduate campus of course opposed this. Brahmans in the city colleges and a few rural colleges were allies of the city college leaders. Leaders on the postgraduate campus, largely

Pune Brahmans (this identity will be discussed later), developed allies among Marathas in the rural colleges and on the postgraduate campus and Brahman teachers from elsewhere in India.

But these resources of powers were only forces in the university's politics if leaders were in a position to appropriate them. This was enabled only, as it is in any government, if leaders held an office in government. This is important – and often not considered much in political analyses – because the offices of government are vested with powers: power to appoint, power to approve, power to veto or reject, power to manipulate, power to legislate and so forth. Neither the appropriation or use of this power is possible unless one is an incumbent of an office in government. This explains why the competition over election to the offices of university government was so important to the university's history of conflict. The allies upon which a leader might rely become an important resource of political power only if that leader occupies an office of government. Axiomatically, to be out of office is to be out of power.

Early in the university's history Brahmans from the city colleges dominated the university because they occupied all important offices of university government. This changed when the 1974 Poona University Act that legally enabled the government of the university, allowed teachers on the postgraduate campus for the first time to compete for critical offices in university government. By the 1980s, Brahman and non-Brahman teachers on the postgraduate campus and their allies in the rural colleges had largely displaced city college Brahmans in university government. The resolution of these contradictions at the moment favours the postgraduate campus. But events in the late 1980s and early 1990s showed that city college Brahmans with allies from conservative national political parties still had the potential to threaten the hegemony of leaders on the postgraduate campus. As long as the organization of the university remains as it is, the nature of these contradictions are likely to provoke conflict for the foreseeable future.

This historical perspective is largely ignored by the university's political leaders. For them, as with many politicians everywhere, the politics is the stuff of the issues and problems of the moment in which they transpire. The history of political conflict in the university suggests otherwise.

Introduction to the University's Politics

To make full sense of the university's politics one has to take into account the historical panorama of caste relations in western India and the gradual transfer of political and economic power from Brahmans to Marathas. This began in the latter decades of the nineteenth century and accelerated after the creation of the state of Maharashtra in 1960. Conflict between these castes penetrated the university in such a way that it reproduced the Brahman caste structure of the university's government while simultaneously attempting to lay the groundwork for a Maratha domination of the university. This condition persists.

Still, there are caveats to an uncritical acceptance of Brahman-Maratha caste differences as the primary explanation for the university's political conflict. Caste relations receive expression most neatly in small village communities. In modern institutions caste becomes augmented with class interests, alliances, patronage, institutional affiliations, and other factors. Leaders of the university's politics support their denial of the significance of caste in its politics by pointing to the inter-caste alliances that characterized the factional fighting in the university, especially since the 1970s. To the extent that inter-caste alliances operated in the university, this notion has some validity.

It is true that Brahmans and Marathas share a long history of conflict in the region. But despite my belief that the caste differences explain best the political conflict in the university, the caste divisions involved in these politics are not clear cut. They never are. And those who disagreed with my emphasis on caste told me so, frequently. But as we shall see, these alliances are not haphazard concoctions. The leaders involved in these conflicts forged alliances with politically motivated intentions that sustained the caste contradiction. The persistent, albeit subtle, patterns to the caste divisions and alliances support an emphasis on caste as the major cause of the conflict. The identities and relations of the castes involved in the conflicts make this clearer.

The Brahman half of the equation in the university's politics comprises different kinds of Brahmans. They represent Chitpavan, Deshasta, Saraswat and Karhada castes. Each of these castes resides primarily in the state of Maharashtra. But Chitpavan Brahmans are identified primarily as Konkanastha[2] or Pune Brahmans. At one time Chitpavan Brahmans dominated the institutions of the city of Pune and today remain important to its ancient tradition as a Brahman stronghold. I shall use the term, Pune Brahman, to refer to Chitpavan Brahmans primarily, but with the caveat that a Pune Brahman also may incorporate other Brahmans who, as we shall see, have been assimilated into the Brahman culture of Poona University and the city of Pune. Other Brahman castes also reside largely in the cities of Maharashtra, including Pune. But their origins are rural and in Pune they often are identified as Maharashtra Brahmans. The last category comprises non-Maharashtra Brahmans. In the university they are referred to as outsider Brahmans.[3] Still, the university's political leaders are *almost* exclusively Brahmans, and most are Pune Brahmans. A few leaders have been Chandraseniya Kayastha Prabhus, or CKPs. They represent a ritually high caste and have a tradition of opposing Brahmans (Gokhale 1988). But to make full sense of the political affiliations of these caste identities it is also necessary to consider the university's institutional and regional contradictions.

Those who dissented to my interpretation of caste as a major factor of the conflict often pointed to the fact that the leaders of the two teams in conflict, the Gang and the Clique as they were known in the university, were Brahman. But the leader of the Gang, which was composed largely of Maharashtra Brahmans, was a Deshasta Brahman. The Gang represented the city colleges and its support came largely from alliances it struck with Pune Brahman personnel primarily in the city colleges. It also had support from some Maharashtra Brahmans in the rural colleges who felt oppressed by the Marathas who operated these colleges. Since Maharashtra and Pune Brahmans dominated the city colleges, the interests of the city colleges were the preteminent concern of the Gang and Brahmans were its logical constituency.

The Clique supported the interests of the postgraduate campus. Its leaders consisted of two Pune Brahmans, a CKP, and several close lieutenants from various castes. As a team the Clique was composed largely of outsider Brahmans and a mixture of individuals from others castes, who were disgruntled with the domination of the campus by city college Brahmans. Other individuals on the postgraduate campus also were allies of the Clique. But for much of the 1980s the Cliques major allies comprised Marathas from the rural colleges. One leader, the Professor as I refer to him, had a sufficiently large enough following of Maratha staffs from the rural colleges, that for much of that decade he dominated the university's politics. The main goal of the Cliques leaders was to assure the ascendancy of the postgraduate campus over the city colleges. Once that happened the caste alliances that the Clique had forged proved to be fragile. At least in part this was because the Brahman leaders of the Clique structured these alliances primarily to serve their private ends. Marathas and outsider Brahmans acceded to them because it appeared at the time to be to their benefit and because they had little choice in selecting leaders. Maratha leadership has not developed in the university, and leadership by outside Brahmans is unthinkable in Poona University.

During this research, informants provided several explanations to account for the political conflict in the university. In 1994-1995, I asked 29 of my most knowledgeable informants what they thought was the major motivation of the political conflict in the university. Two major explanations emerged.

Some argued that interests motivated these politics. These interests were concerned with elections to government offices, employment, appointments, service contracts, program development, and the like. Others argued that the politics were motivated by caste antagonisms between Brahmans and non-Brahmans that were built into the university's structure and organization. Some explanations included both conditions, but emphasized one over the other. A few argued that they were equally important.

In Table 1 below I attempt to make sense of these differences as they were perceived by some of those who were involved in the university's politics. There are a number of ways to denote the caste affiliations of adherents to each explanation. As noted, Brahmans were represented by several categories. Non-Brahmans refer primarily to Marathas. But it also includes other non-Brahmans castes as well, such as Jains, CKPs and other middle castes. It is not my purpose here to weigh statistically the responses of these categories. Instead, it is sufficient to present how 29 knowledgeable informants explained the causes of the conflict. It is worth noting that the 7 politicians among those 29 informants were most likely to deny caste as a cause of the conflict and emphasize other issues instead. Marathas and non-Brahmans, on the other hand, were most likely to emphasize caste as the cause of the conflict. Note also that within all caste categories or a caste emphasis prevailed over issues or an emphasis on issues as the most common explanation.

Those who emphasize caste as the underlying factor in the university's political conflict point to the ancient history of hostilities between Brahmans and non-Brahmans, in particular Marathas.[4] They assert that these hostilities have been carried over into the structure of the university. Almost all of the university's politicians reject the prominence of caste as the source of the conflict. They point as proof of their position to the inter-caste alliances that were commonly

Table 1

Categories	Caste	Issues	Caste-issues	Issues-caste	Equal
All categories	7	7	10	3	2
Brahmans	3	4	7	1	0
Non-Brahmans	1	2	3	1	1
Marathas	3	1	1	0	1
Politicians	0	3	2	1	1

established by different leaders in pursuit of their goals. But, as noted, there is a coherence to these alliances that suggests strongly that they were formed with caste considerations clearly in mind.

The explanation that related best to my data and provided sharpest insight into the history of the university's political conflict indicated that caste lay at the heart of this conflict. This is not because caste is synonymous with Indian social organization and penetrates every Indian social structure. Neither is it because almost all behaviors and practices in India can be reduced to caste (which does not mean that caste is unimportant). Neither is it because individuals involved in the conflicts commonly used caste designations, such as the Marathas, Brahmans, Chitpavans Konkanasthas, and "outsiders", to identify leaders and others who were politically invested. Instead, caste, more than other factors, situated the university's politics in a context that documented *historical contradictions between various categories of Brahmans and non-Brahmans, in particular, Marathas, that continues to be worked out in the university's politics.* Historically, since the last quarter of the nineteenth century, Maratha influence, leadership, and political economic power has replaced Brahman leadership and influence in every institution in Maharashtra (Sirsikar 1995) except Poona University. The dialectic that political agents are working out in the politics of the university is significant because Poona University is the last bastion of Brahman power and influence in the state of Maharashtra.

Still, leaders involved in the day-to-day fights also were correct when they asserted that the politics were issue oriented. They thought themselves involved in fights over immediate issues that were grounded in their overarching concerns over the well-being of the university. But these leaders also overlooked the historical dimension of this conflict. For the leaders and others who were engaged in the university's politics the practicing ethnographic present includes only the late 1960s to the present. But from the perspective of the historical ethnographic present which this work takes, the contradictions in caste that underlie the political fights in the university are at least 350 years old. They are part of a rich tradition of caste conflict between non-Brahmans and Brahmans in western India (Omvedt 1976; O' Hanlon 1985; Gore 1989). The conflict that is a result of these caste contradictions has been recurrent in Poona University since it was first conceived in 1924, about 80 years ago.

Notes

1. Maratha is a complicated term. It incorporates other castes, such as Khunbis, some of whom identify themselves as Marathas and other who do not. I used the term here as it was used in the vernacular of those who were involved in the politics which this research addresses. They did not make such fine distinctions. For an excellent analysis of the idea, Maratha, see O'Hanlon (1985).
2. The adjective Konkanastha refers to the Konkan, a coastal region just south of Mumbai. Several centuries ago Chitpavan Brahmans from this region began to migrate into the region that became Maharashtra and the city of Pune. By the eighteenth century they had become a dominant force in the region's politics.
3. Dalits or Harijans, also referred to as untouchables or scheduled castes have not been important in the university's politics. But due to changes in the law in the 1990s, Dalits began to be awarded faculty positions on the postgraduate campus. This will be considered in Chapter 8.
4. Marathas are an ancient caste in that part of western India that became the state of Maharashtra in 1960. They reasserted their identity to provide Marathas an ideological source of political power to challenge the domination of Chitpavan Brahmans in the last quarter of the nineteenth century (Omvedt 1976; O'Hanlon 1985; Sirisikar 1995).

Dramatis Personae: Leaders, Agents, and Affiliations

1. *Chancellor*: The Governor of the state of Maharashtra and a political appointee of the Central government in Delhi. He appoints Vice-Chancellors and Pro-Vice Chancellors and is the ultimate source of appeal on university issues.

2. *Vice-Chancellor*: The principal executive office, of Poona University. Except for 1978-1984 and 1989-1995 he was always a Brahman.

3. *Executive Council*: The principle and most important authority of the university. From the mid-1960s, it was always dominated by one of the university's major political teams.

4. *The Gang*: The dominant political team from about the mid-1960s until about 1978. It represented the interests of Pune's city colleges.

5. *CC Leader*: The Brahman leader of the Gang.

6. *The Clique*: The dominant political team in the university from about 1978 to the present. It represented the interests of the postgraduate campus.

7. *Campus Leader*: The first Brahman leader of the Clique.

8. *Professor*: A Brahman who by the 1980s had built massive support in rural colleges and became the single-most powerful agent in the university. He allied with the Clique around 1981 and became one of its leaders.

9. *Aspirant*: A non-Brahman (CKP) leader of the Clique and, subsequently, Vice-Chancellor.

10. *Brahman Lobby*: A loosely knit and amorphous coalition of Pune Brahman dissidents on and off the campus, who opposed the Clique vehemently.

11. *VC*: the Vice-Chancellor (1984-1989). A Brahman who represented either the interests of the city colleges, the postgraduate campus, or his own depending on one's interpretation.

12. *Maverick*: A Brahman who rejected caste affiliation. He was an independent agent who represented primarily his own interests. Although some identified him as a member of the Clique, he was extremely antagonistic to the Campus Leader, Aspirant and the VC.

13. *Teachers Union*: A college-based organization that represented primarily the interests of the rural colleges and was largely Brahman in composition.

I

Chapter

The Setting: The Postgraduate Campus and Colleges

The Postgraduate Campus

The postgraduate campus of Poona University sprawls over 409 acres of wooded land on the northwest edge of the city of Pune. A high arch bearing the name, "Poona University", introduces the entrance to the campus. About 30 yards beyond the entrance and past a row of gnarled and towering banyan trees, a large map mounted on a billboard shows the layout of the campus. At this point the road divides and assumes the form of an angular tear drop as it winds through the campus.

Compared to the deforestation of much of the surrounding countryside the campus vegetation is conspicuous. In the rainy season the landscape – fields, shrubs, trees – is thick and verdant. Abruptly, when the dry season begins much of the verdure fades and the campus acquires a dusty beige ambience. At this time only the carefully tended gardens and lawns of the central administration building – or main building as it is referred to – retain their lushness.

The main building is located about halfway, at the bulb of the tear drop, on the road that begins at the entrance to the university. It marks the functional centre of the campus. The British constructed it and from 1868 to 1947 it served as the governor's mansion and seat of government of the Bombay

Presidency in the monsoon season. It is a large, unusual, rambling and stately structure that defies obvious architectural classification. It has two elegant porticoes and an 80-foot high campanile that is crowned by a brilliantly painted, open metal cupola embellished with a tall flagstaff. In front, across from its major portico and broad driveway, its meticulously tended garden and floral displays are locally famous. Behind it an expansive lawn provides space for Sunday picnics for visitors, a pleasant place to stroll or sit anytime, and the location for the annual convocation. The area around the main building bustles during business hours with people and traffic.

This imposing edifice served as the university's central administration building for 37 years. As the university expanded it became inadequate. In 1986 a new building was completed about 300 yards northwest of the old one. It is starkly modern and efficient, composed of cavernous work spaces and large offices. It now houses most of the university's records and administrative personnel. The Vice-Chancellor, the chief political and administrative officer of the university, retains an office in the main building.

Most of the postgraduate departments are within easy walking distance of the main building. But a few, such as journalism and modern European languages, are located in Pune. The departments of archaeology and linguistics are housed on the Deccan College Campus, an affiliate college of the university, on the edge of the city.

The campus also accommodates several specialized centres of study concerned with advanced studies in Sanskrit, material science, and solid state physics. The Educational and Media Research Centre (EMRC) trains students in all aspects of the field of television. Its major role is to produce educational videos for the Countrywide Classroom Project sponsored by the UGC. Much of this production derives from faculty research projects. In addition, the campus is home to several national research facilities, such as the Inter-University Centre of Astronomy and Astrophysics (IUCCA).

In 1985-1986, the ethnographic present for much of this work, Poona University comprised a postgraduate campus and 173 urban and rural colleges in which approximately 4,500 teachers instructed 1,20,000 students. The postgraduate campus had about 300 faculty and 3,500 students seeking masters and/or doctoral degrees. Of the 173 colleges, 48 were in Pune. The remaining 125 are located in the cities, town, and villages throughout the university's five districts that constitute that part of the Deccan Plateau that is the state of Maharashtra.

In 1995, the university had 202 colleges and 1,80,000 students. In the city 74 colleges were located; 128 were in rural areas.[1] The postgraduate campus was home to 36 departments. These departments enrolled about 500 Ph D, 325 masters, and 4,800 postgraduate students, who were taught by about 340 teachers. About 10 per cent of these students came from most of India's other 22 states. In 1985-1986, 105 foreign students attended. They came primarily from Africa and Southeast Asia. The foreign student population increased to 463 in 1993-1994 and to 611 in 1994-1995.

Teachers

The postgraduate campus employs around 340 teachers, almost all of whom believe that the university is a very desirable place to work. A teacher is awarded the equivalent of tenure after serving in a two-year probationary period. A wise teacher will strive to endear himself/herself to the head and other powerful members of the employing department. Scholarship is not always the deciding factor in awarding a permanent appointment. Some, more aggressive scholars lament what they perceive to be an inordinate number of teachers who teach badly and do not engage in research. Nonetheless, the university maintains an excellent reputation for scholarship.

Teachers attribute this reputation largely to the fact that, as they assert, "the university works." By this they mean that compared to other Indian universities, education and the academic enterprise go on day in and day out on the postgraduate campus. Faith in that mantra was badly shaken in 1989 when it appeared that the postgraduate campus would succumb to the politicization that has marked other Indian universities. But, to the credit of its teachers and administration, the campus came through that period without undue intrusion into its academic activities by outside political, caste, and religious antagonists. Except for the events of 1989, even the political conflict that has been so much a part of its history has not interfered much with the work of its faculty and students. But since 1989 political party influence has been more intrusive in university government.

Teachers on the postgraduate campus do not suffer much from the tyranny of department heads. This is a nearly universal complaint in other Indian universities. In Poona University, department heads are usually professors and, most commonly, males. If a head is the only professor in the department, as is common in small departments, he may make sure that no other professorships are allocated to the department. In larger departments with more than one professor, seniority may prevail as the basis for awarding headships, or they may be bitterly contested.

Even though department heads are far less dictatorial than those in most other Indian universities, teachers often resent the heads of their departments because of the considerable authority and power they exert over department personnel and affairs. The Vice-Chancellor has a tendency now rotate the headship every three years in departments with more than one professor. The University Act that establishes the structure and statutes for university government provides for this option. But it is not normative practice. Vice-Chancellors tend to enforce the rule when it suits their interests. This policy is an aspect of power relations in the university. It is one way that Vice-Chancellors can acquire support and squash resistance. Department heads are also important players in the university's politics because of the representation they have on some of the university's administrative and political boards and authorities.

Campus Community

The university provides accommodation on campus for the families of 118 teachers (about 40 per cent of the teaching staff) at concession rate that is 10 per cent of a teacher's monthly salary. This is a remarkably low rent for the area. The university's accommodations are very desirable and the envy of teachers of city colleges. But they have their drawbacks.

The campus is a tight little community. There is little privacy. People know their neighbours intimately, their quirks, foibles, pastimes, teaching practices, research abilities, political affiliations, and the like. Visitors to the flats are scrutinized closely to assess relationships. Gossip is rampant and spreads with the speed of the human voice. Envy of those who have more things, a new car or telephone, is common and is bound to elicit comments regarding the devious ways the desiderata was procured, for how could it be otherwise, given the teachers' salaries? Very little goes unnoticed and considerably more is said than needs to be. The unrestrained flow of information about events in the university is a significant part of the university politics and political conflict; almost every political action and event is known by everyone interested almost immediately. Many families long to be off the campus for the sake of privacy, but they cannot surrender one of the university's biggest perks.

Colleges

English is the medium of instruction in most Indian universities, and this is so for Poona University also, in particular on the postgraduate campus and in the city colleges. Colleges are privately owned. Most are managed by some trust, organization, cooperative, caste or religious community. Quality depends on the commitment of managements to invest resources in education. Many, especially rural colleges and city "slum colleges" as they are called by some on the postgraduate campus, were started by politicians for political purposes. Rural colleges in particular are run by the Congress Party and Congress Party politicians, largely Maratha today, use them to promote their political ambitions (Rosenthal 1977; Lele 1984). The overwhelming number of rural colleges are owned and managed by Marathas and related to the sugar cooperatives that they operate and through which the Marathas have acquired pre-eminent political economic clout in Maharashtra (Baviskar 1980; Attwood 1992). The majority of rural teachers, perhaps 50 per cent, are Brahman. Of the remainder about 30 per cent are Maratha. But as Maratha teachers increase in number they are gradually replacing Brahmans (Bhoite 1987).

Most colleges provide only a BA or BSc degree, although some have specialized postgraduate programs. Most of these offer masters degrees; a few offer the Ph D. Among both the urban and rural colleges some are very good and some are very poor, such as Pune's slum colleges. Most are adequate by Indian standards. A few rural colleges are just shells and exist primarily on paper by which they were approved and provide a minimal education. These colleges sustain themselves because there is a surfeit of students, many of whom are too poor to matriculate to a better college. Some bogus colleges exist purely for the money that their managements earn through fees. Any degree from one of them will be of dubious quality.

I visited 12 colleges, 6 city and 6 rural, that were in some way important to the university's politics. To give some sense of their disposition I will introduce two city colleges whose personnel were politically active and then generalize more broadly about rural colleges

City Colleges

Fergusson College is Pune's oldest and most venerable college. Several of the university's important politicians have come from Fergusson and other personnel have been, at times, politically active in university affairs. It has been in existence for over 100 years and the prestigious Deccan Educational Society manages it. It provides a full array of liberal arts and science courses and it is well equipped with modern educational technology. Instruction takes place on an extensive campus with tree lined streets and walks. Teachers hold their classes in imposing but attractive stone buildings that date back to the Raj. Several teashops, meal hotels, bookstalls, restaurants, tailors, hairstylists (for males) and other service shops operate outside the campus for several blocks along Fergusson Road. The area is a gathering place for Fergusson students as well as those from nearby colleges and the postgraduate campus. The downtown branch of the postgraduate campus is located nearby. In 1983 an eating establishment opened that was modelled after a western fast food outlet. Others have opened since. They serve an Indian fast food cuisine, such as vegetable and mutton burgers. *Pav bhaji*, a vegetarian sloppy Joe, was a rage in 1994. Still, they remain somewhat less popular than the more established eateries. This area is the closest to the western idea of a college campus area that exists in Pune.

Symbiosis College is one of Pune's newest colleges. An ex-principal of Fergusson College established it in the 1980s. Until around 1978 he was one of the university's most effective and important political agents. We will meet him later as the CC (City College) Leader.

Symbiosis College sits on a hill overlooking Pune. It is conspicuous by its modernity when it is compared to the weighty stone elegance of Fergusson College and the single modest reference to its name on the arch that spans its entrance and understates its reputation and venerable status. Symbiosis is compact, built of concrete and glass. It displays its names boldly – ostentatiously – on a stone wall at the entrance and on other buildings that are visible from the road in front. Most dramatic is the facade of its main building: "SYMBIOSIS " in large red letters is adorned on all sides by paintings of the flags of 50 nations. Its curriculum specializes in commerce, and it caters to foreign students.

The college is well endowed, has a reputation for excellence, and foreign students pay premium fees to attend. It has modern facilities, a good library, and a qualified staff that provides quality education. The Director – in this work, the CC Leader – also has a reputation as a good administrator and educator, even among those who were his political antagonists. He does not interfere in the operation of the college for venal or other personal motives as some other directors do in institutions of lesser quality.

Pune has a long tradition of providing educational excellence through its colleges, and their teachers are proud of it. By 1994 this was changing. The slum colleges, for example, are a recent phenomenon. As Pune's population grew dramatically in the 1980s and 1990s, colleges of lesser quality began to be opened by unscrupulous "educators" who were more interested in the money to be earned. Teachers in the city colleges, as on the postgraduate campus, tend to be middle class, well paid, and largely dedicated to pedagogical pursuits. The cost of living in Pune is high and housing is scarce and costly. Teachers in the city colleges do not have the advantage of subsidized housing as on the postgraduate campus. Many city college teachers resent the perks that teachers on the postgraduate campus receive, which also include higher salaries and lower teaching loads. They suffer from what they perceive to be a relative deprivation in status, prestige and reward relative to the postgraduate campus.

Most city college teachers feel that they are equal in scholarship to the teachers on the postgraduate campus. They also believe that the education and research that take place in the colleges is superior to much that occurs on the campus. They would like better recognition for their scholarship. Since the political activity on the postgraduate campus receives considerable attention in the local press, some city college teachers also resent what they believe is a lack of dedication to scholarship by the postgraduate teachers. They also lament the vicarious loss of respect for teachers in general among the city's population that they believe these politics induce.

Rural Colleges

Maratha-based educational societies and politicians operate and manage the vast majority of rural colleges. In these colleges Marathi competes with English as the medium of education. Marathas represent the caste that predominates numerically in the countryside. As noted, they also control political and economic power in Maharashtra. Still, only a few of the older rural colleges are sufficiently endowed with wealth and concerned managements to approach the educational status of many city colleges. The status of the newer rural colleges does not compare, although recall that there is a corresponding decline in quality in the newer city colleges also. University government knows that many rural colleges, like city slum colleges, are of marginal quality. But it affiliates them with the university in part to help provide resources to upgrade them.

Though rural college management is largely Maratha, rural college teachers, as noted, tend to be Brahman. Teaching is a traditional Brahman occupation in India. Marathas traditionally have been farmers and not much interested in higher education. But as they began to see economic and social advantages in higher education over the last few decades, Marathas became more interested in it. Now, as Maratha teachers increase in number, they are slowly replacing Brahmans.

The vast majority of rural college teachers hold only a masters degree. It is a stipulation of employment. There is little in college teaching to stimulate them intellectually. It may even be discouraged because it detracts from other expectations that college managements have for their employees, such as participating in political campaigns or raising funds for management-sponsored candidates. Teachers lecture; even on the postgraduate campus seminars are uncommon. College teachers especially make few, if any digressions, from minimal standards required by the syllabus.

The attitude of rural college teachers regarding education and their roles as educators is poor. While college teachers may be perceived by local people as purveyors of necessary knowledge, they are not much respected. An indeterminate, but large number is not considered by students, colleagues, and knowledgeable members of the community to be either good teachers or dedicated to their profession. Those who are and who may speak out on issues may lose standing in the community if they challenge acceptable norms. The day of the revered guru is over. Rural teachers often think of their academic work as a perfunctory obligation to be dispensed with as quickly as possible so that more remunerative activities can be pursued.

Economically, rural college teachers comprise an elite category. They and city college teachers receive an income that is the equivalent of a lecturer's salary on the postgraduate campus. This is a substantial amount in rural areas where the cost of living is considerably lower than in Pune. More than half the teachers also have other employment. Many are self-employed as shopkeepers or farmers. Others work as insurance agents or vehicle salesmen. Some coach students to pass examinations and may write study guides that can be approved for use and sale to students. A few may translate textbooks from English to Marathi. In general, rural college teachers have a very comfortable life.

Students in the city colleges are better motivated than their rural counterparts. Still, rural students are rapidly learning to comprehend the importance of a college education for employment and economic advancement in their changing world. But in the strangulated job market that students confront, recourse to "unfair means" is common. This includes cheating in examinations, paying a bribe to attain entrance to a college or to alter a grade, and threats to teachers. These problems are topics of national debate. They are also problems in the university, especially in the rural colleges. It is also not uncommon for rural college teachers who serve as examination proctors to be intimidated by students to overlook mass copying in an examination. Some who have attempted to enforce examination rules against cheating have been physically attacked. Yet, they also attest that most students are honest, and that it is only a few "hooligans" who create most of the problems.

Notes

1. The university's postgraduate departments and the dates when they were established include: Sanskrit and Prakrit Language (1949), Marathi, Politics and Public Administration, Psychology, Sociology, Chemistry, Zoology, Mathematics, and Geography (1950), Physics (1952), Geology (1955), Modern European Languages, Library & Information Sciences (1958), Archaeology (1959), Hindi, Linguistics (1960), English (1961), Centre for Advanced Study in Sanskrit, Centre for Advanced Study in Agricultural Economics, Defense Studies, Communication and Journalism, (1964), Philosophy, law (1965), History (1969), Statistics (1978), Anthropology (1979), Microbiology (1982), Electronic Science, Communication Studies, Commerce and Business management (1985), Economics (1987), Computer Sciences (1988), Performing Arts, Continuing Adult Education and Extension, Ayurvedic Medicine, Education and Extension (1990), Instrumentation Science (1992), Biotechnology (1993).

II
Chapter
Background to University Government and Politics

Introduction

In 1924 the Bombay University Reform Committee recommended the establishment of a new university in each of the linguistic regions that comprised the Bombay Presidency: Sind, Gujarat, Maharashtra, and Karnataka. Pune was selected for the Maharashtra University because, as noted, it was the seat of British government during the monsoon and a centre of intellectual, educational, social, and political activities. It also had a reputation as a Brahman city, and its prestigious colleges catered to this clientele.

The recommendation was resisted by many in Pune, including the Deccan Educational Society. The society remains a powerful organization and was responsible for founding many of Pune's best colleges, such as Deccan and Fergusson colleges. It and other foes perceived the university to be a threat to the autonomy of the Pune colleges.

Once Pune was selected as the site for the university, issues emerged and demanded attention. A major issue concerned whether the university would be a residential teaching university with postgraduate courses offered on a separate campus, or an affiliating university that merely granted higher degrees in recognition of courses and programs provided by the colleges. Protracted debates over this matter, the freedom struggle, and the second World War delayed the opening of the university until 1949.

Poona University was established with a postgraduate campus in Pune under the authority provided by the University Act of 1948. It opened and accepted its first students on February 10, 1949. The 20 colleges and 7 research institutions that initially comprised the university were incorporated as two separate administrative entities promulgated in the Poona University Act, 1948 and sustained in each University Act thereafter in 1974 and 1994.[1] The Acts designate the city colleges and research institutions as *constituent* colleges of the university. Rural colleges are *affiliated* to the university. This distinction is more than terminological. The city colleges enjoy greater administrative autonomy within the university than the rural colleges regarding matters such as curriculum and fiscal responsibility. Prior to 1974 city colleges were also considerably more influential in university political affairs. For example, early in the history of the university they insisted on and received their special status as constituent institutions of the university. By the late 1970s city college influence had waned and influence from the rural colleges was ascendant.

Regardless of this turn and conflict over college influence in the university's politics, city and rural colleges today are subordinate to the postgraduate campus. Political power and authority over the university is firmly entrenched in the hands of agents on the postgraduate campus. Personnel from the colleges who engage in university government come to it to participate in the university's authorities, boards, and committees that comprise university government. Decisions and policies that emanate from the campus can affect the colleges strongly.

University Government

The structure of government at Poona University is not appreciably different from that of other Indian universities (Tickoo 1980). In India almost all universities are defined by a University Act which authorizes their existence. In effect, the government of Poona University is a structure of authorities and boards whose offices are occupied by incumbents who are elected to them (Figure 1).[2] As a result of occupying an elected office, incumbents are vested with the power and authority of that office to make authoritative decisions and enact policies that are binding on the managements of the rural and city colleges and the administration of the postgraduate campus. The political fighting in the university has been largely over access to seats on these authorities.

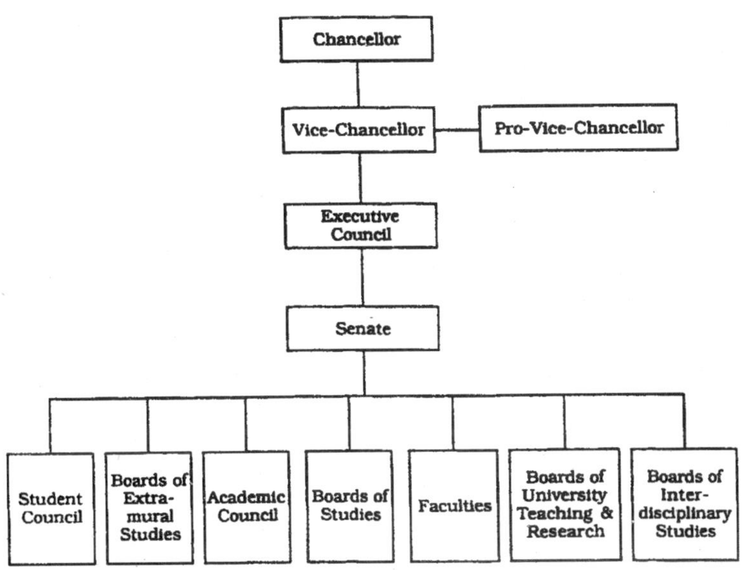

Figure 1 : The Structure of the University (according to University Act 1974 [corrected 1/4/79])

The offices of Chancellor and Vice-Chancellor are at the apex of this structure. The Chancellor is the governor of the state and a political appointee of the Central government in Delhi. He serves largely as a mediator or arbiter of disputes in the university. His major role is to appoint the Vice-

Chancellor and Pro-Vice-Chancellor, each from a slate of three names submitted to him at the appropriate time by a university committee.

The Vice-Chancellor is the principal executive and administrative officer of the university.[3] He represents it at official functions in India and abroad. He is *ex-officio* chairman of most the authorities that comprise university government. He also can be deeply involved in the university's politics, sometimes to his personal detriment.

As noted, the first Pro-Vice-Chancellor was appointed in 1985. In the absence of the Vice-Chancellor the Pro-Vice Chancellor is charged to represent him. Beyond that the powers and duties of the office are ambiguous.

State government agents who are involved in matters of education in Maharashtra occupy five seats. The remaining 16 are filled by one department head on the postgraduate campus who is elected by other heads from among themselves, two principals elected from the senate, two teachers elected from the senate, seven other individuals elected from the senate who represent its non-academic categories, one dean elected by the deans from among themselves, and three persons who represent the faculties and are elected by the Academic Council. University politicians covet seats on the Executive Council and contest for them hotly. This is because it is involved literally in all university affairs and business, especially the allocation of university resources.

The Executive Council also works closely with the Vice-Chancellor. For a Vice-Chancellor to be effective in managing university affairs and gain agreement with his decisions he must establish a coalition in the Executive Council. If the Executive Council is split into factions, or in chronic disagreement with the Vice-Chancellor, this can be difficult, if not impossible.

The Senate is the most ecumenical of the university's authorities. It also is the largest and numbers in the hundreds. The unwieldy size of Indian university senates is a matter of concern in higher education (Tickoo 1980) and Poona University's Senate is no exception. It recruits its membership from among university teachers, principals, department heads, teachers of secondary schools, university students, registered graduates (alumni) and constituencies that represent local businesses, political associations and parties, and professional associations. The latter three categories elect members from among themselves who are formally registered with the university. The Senate is the principal authority for all considerations regarding financial and budgetary appropriations related to the university. Most of its functions are advisory in nature. But others, such as making, amending, or repealing the statutes of the University Act are formidable. People refer to the Senate as the watchdog of the university.

The Academic Council is the principal authority for the university's academic affairs. Its primary task is to establish standards for teaching, research, and examinations. It recruits members from the postgraduate campus and colleges. College principals dominate its membership.

Teachers, lay people, and students who represent related disciplinary fields of study, such as the natural sciences, fine arts, social sciences, and the like comprise the faculties. Faculties recruit their members from the Senate, Academic Council, and Boards of Studies. Their membership tends to be dominated by college personnel. The primary function of the faculties is to elect a dean who represents each disciplinary field to the administration. Deans may become very active political agents.

Finally, a Board of Study exists for each subject taught in the university. The main function of a Board of Study is to establish a syllabus for each course that is taught in the subject the Board represents. The purpose of this is to standardize course offerings in each discipline among departments in the colleges and on the postgraduate campus. Boards of Studies tend to be dominated by college personnel. Any particular Board will be composed of not more that ten heads of the concerned departments in the colleges, the heads of departments on the postgraduate campus, two teachers, and three lay persons with special knowledge of the subject.

Electoral Processes

The above university authorities represent those that are important to its politics. The University Act and its statutes prescribe the process of recruitment to them. The Vice-Chancellor is *ex-officio* head of each authority and each also includes other *ex-officio* representatives who are appointed from local and state governments and other specified agencies and associations. Most incumbents, however, are elected and recruited from a variety of specific constituencies, most of which represent university personnel (see Figure 2). Among non-university constitu-encies only those individuals who are associated with a constituency that is registered with and thereby recognized by the university may compete for a seat on an authority. In most instances they are elected from among the members of that constituency, although in some instances represen-tatives to the authorities rotate among members of the constituency. Non-university personnel are recruited from alumni, state and local government, local business and industries, higher secondary education, trade unions, cooperative societies and donors to the university.

Among the university authorities, the Boards of Studies are especially important to political recruitment. They are the source of ingress to higher authorities for teachers. Heads of colleges and postgraduate departments may elect representatives from among themselves or rotate among themselves to seats on the Boards of Studies. But teachers who wish to enter the political arena or, more likely, who are politically desirable to one of the university's faction may be "co-opted"; that is, the members of a Board of Study elect the individual to it. Of course, this means that the members of a Board of Study must be allied to one of the factions in university government. From this point of ingress individuals may stand for election to the faculties and Academic Council. If leaders of one or another faction control the votes on those boards, an individual stands a good chance of being elected, and from there he or she may move on to other, higher authorities.

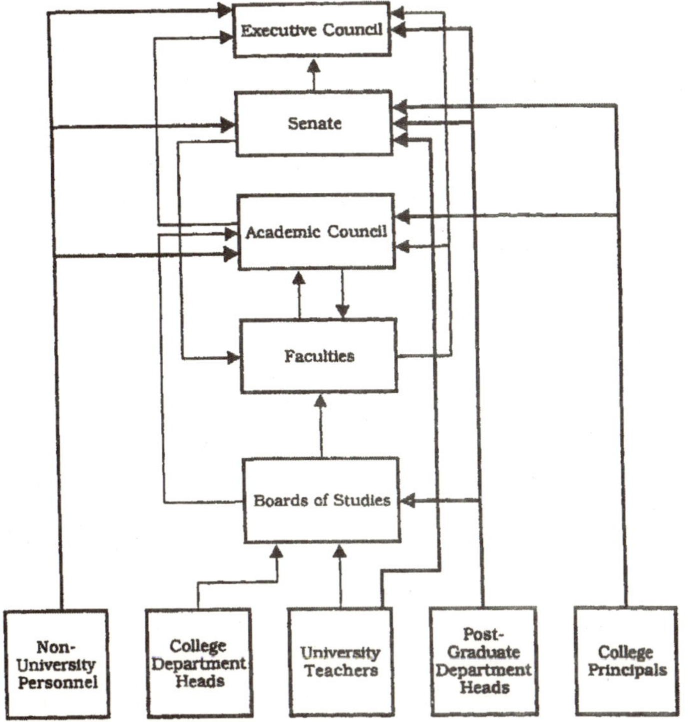

Figure 2 : Recruitment and voting pathways

This figure excludes ex-officio members. It includes some appointed members, although most are elected. It ignores proportions of representation (line density is for clarity only)

Voting for representatives on the university's various authorities is not effected through the universal suffrage of the university's teachers. Individuals are elected to an authority by the members of that or another authority. An individual may also hold a seat on more than one authority. When elections to the various authorities are held, they follow immediately one after the other, giving time of course for individuals to campaign. Thus, an individual may move in short order, a matter of weeks, to higher authorities, including a seat on the Executive Council.

Competition among the politicians and their followers for seats on these authorities is intense, for whoever controls the votes cast by members of these authorities controls the university's government. For example, in 1986 the university's most powerful political agent, the Professor, controlled voting majorities on 48 of the 52 Boards of Studies and the Senate, as well as enjoying support from many department heads and college principals. In effect, the Professor and his allies ran the university.

Power Relations

The contradictions that have generated so much conflict in Poona University can be understood only in the history of the power relations between its colleges and the castes they represent. For example, during the years since the inception of the 1974 Act rural Maratha colleges have played a much more significant role in university politics. As leaders on the postgraduate campus and in the city colleges began to see advantages in seeking allies in the rural colleges, management and teachers in the rural colleges began to see their active participation in university government as a lever against the domination of the university by the city colleges and postgraduate campus. This interplay has reshaped gradually the nature of university government. But the main harbinger of change and conflict in the university over the last 20 years has been the Poona University Act of 1974.

The 1974 Act altered power relations between political agents with unexpected results. Some agents maintain that the 1974 Act was a marvelous document of checks and balances and precluded internecine political fighting. Actually it was the provisions of the Act and their creative interpretation by various agents that permitted the contradictions in the university to surface vigorously and foment much of the conflict since 1974. This is because the University Acts determined which personnel are eligible to be recruited to offices on university authorities and, with the power invested in them, to play in the game of university politics.

The 1948 Act, for example, did not permit personnel from the postgraduate campus to serve on the Executive Council. For 25 years personnel from the city colleges dominated the Executive Council and office of Vice-Chancellor, the university's most powerful authorities, and therefore university government. The 1974 Act changed all that. It permitted postgraduate teachers to contest for seats on the Executive Council. Considerable input from people on the postgraduate campus into the legislation that enabled the 1974 Act accomplished this. Much of the recent history of conflict in the university derives from attempts of agents who represent caste alignments and interests in the city and rural colleges and postgraduate campus to acquire seats on university authorities. With the inauguration of the 1974 Act, conflict in the university became more deeply embedded in contradictions of caste, region and institution that comprise the university.

Caste and the University

The structure and location of castes and the percentage of caste affiliation within the region that became the state of

Maharashtra have not changed appreciably over the last century or so. Brahmans continue to make up about 5 per cent of the population. Marathas, a fairly recent caste as we shall see, account for about 45 per cent. The remaining 50 per cent is distributed among a variety of middle castes, schedule castes, and tribes. These figures tend to be inverted in the university, although there is some variation institutionally.

On the postgraduate campus Brahmans, local and outsider, comprise about 60 per cent of the teachers and Marathas account for about 6 per cent. The remaining 34 per cent comprised a variety of middle castes and members of other communities, such as Muslims, Jains, and CKPs. In the city colleges local Brahman categories provide most of the teachers and management. Among these, Chitpavans hold a more elite status than either the Deshasta or Saraswat Brahmans.

Caste organization in the rural colleges is more complicated. Those rural colleges that have contributed personnel to the university's politics represent managements that are either Brahman, especially the rural Deshasta Brahmans, or Marathas. Other communities, such as scheduled castes, may be politically active in a local context, such as agitating at a college for reservations or social justice. But they are not important in those fights over control of the university's government. Until the early 1970s Brahman-managed colleges were more politically significant than those managed by Marathas. That changed as Maratha economic and political influence increased in the countryside (Carter 1974; Rosenthal 1977; Baviskar 1980; Attwood 1992). Today the overwhelming majority of rural colleges are managed by Marathas although Brahmans, locals and outsiders, continue to provide most of the teachers.

Unlike the city colleges where some elite colleges, such as Fergusson and Deccan Colleges (see Appendix, Episode

Three for politics at the Deccan College), predated the postgraduate campus, almost all the 125 rural colleges were established after the postgraduate campus. Only a few of these colleges had an elite status, and this was always less than that of the city colleges. Maratha college personnel consider those in the city colleges to be rude and haughty and contend that they have not been treated well by the city colleges. As a result they look to the postgraduate campus for help and assistance. Yet, they complain that the personnel from the postgraduate campus are also elitist. This perception is not entirely unfounded. It is embedded in ancient class antagonisms in western India that originated in the middle of the seventeenth century and culminated in the 1870s and 1880s. At that time non-Brahmans challenged seriously the cultural hegemony and political and economic domination of the region's Brahmans. This history is essential to understanding the caste contradictions that predominate in university politics.

Historical Prologue

In the middle of the seventeenth century, Shivaji, a warrior leader of the Sudra, or farmer *varna*[4] rallied Brahmans and non-Brahmans alike to revolt against the Mughals who had ruled the Deccan region for several centuries. Shivaji defeated the Mughals in a series of brilliant victories (recall the significance of Shivaji as a symbol in Episode Five). While his political credit was high Shivaji, with the questionable help of a Brahman priest, had his status elevated and legitimated in the Kshatriya varna to become king (Duff 1990 [1863]). His claim to Kshatriya status and ultimate investiture as king was not well accepted by Brahmans at the time. But they did not challenge it, and non-Brahmans ignored it. This event would have broad effects later (O'Hanlon 1985).

After Shivaji died, antagonisms developed between heirs to his throne and Brahmans who previously migrated from the Konkan, a coastal district south of Mumbai. These were the Chitpavan Brahmans or Pune Brahmans as they are referred to more commonly in the region today. Through shrewd manipulations, members of the Chitpavan caste managed to become prime ministers, or Peshwas, to Shivaji's heirs. Gradually Shivaji's descendants lost power to the Chitpavan Peshwas. In the eighteenth century, on the eve of the British incursion into the region, real government power and authority were firmly ensconced in the Peshwas and their cabinets, which also were overwhelmingly Chitpavan.

Then as now the Chitpavan caste, along with Brahman castes that are native to the region, the Deshasta, Saraswat, and Karhada Bahamans, comprised only about 5 per cent of the region's total population. And among these castes the Chitpavan Brahmans were then and continue to be a minority (Johnson 1970). Still, Brahmans from these castes constituted about 20 per cent of the region's urban population. In Pune, urban Brahmans were overwhelmingly Chitpavan, and they were firmly in control of the region's cultural, educational, political, and religious institutions. They retained control through marriage among themselves (Johnson 1970; Gokhale 1988).

In rural areas non-Brahman peasants comprised the vast majority of the population. They were subjected to Brahman landlords and money lenders, usually non-Chitpavan, who effectively relegated them to a condition of debt peonage (Cashman 1975). Gradually Brahman cultural hegemony became complete and was underwritten by their political and economic domination in the region (Omvedt 1976; Zelliot 1982; O'Hanlon 1985). As a result, Brahmans effectively excluded non-Brahmans from positions of influence and access to them, such as education. It was not until the middle of the nineteenth century that a non-Brahman leadership developed to lead an anti-Brahman resistance movement (Omvedt 1976; O'Hanlon 1985).

In the second decade of the nineteenth century the British took control of the region. Although they distrusted the Brahmans, especially the Chitpavans, they also recognized their talents. In order to secure Chitpavan assistance in their government they took various steps to win over and recruit them. But they also took steps to curtail their power and influence and growing resistance to the Raj. Despite this the Chitpavan Brahmans made the most of available opportunities. By the middle of the nineteenth century the Chitpavans again acquired political power and reestablished their influence far in excess of their numbers (Omvedt 1976; Zelliot 1982; O'Hanlon 1985; Duff 1990 [1863])

In the latter decades of the nineteenth century non-Brahman intellectuals in Pune organized a political and cultural movement that challenged Brahman influence. They announced their claim to descent from Shivaji, elevated him as a symbol of their identity, announced their status in the Maratha caste, and demanded the acknow-ledgement of Marathas in the Kshatriya varna. Most importantly, increasing numbers of others in non-Brahman castes began to shun their previous caste status and claim identity as Marathas. Over the years this swelled the numbers of the Maratha caste considerably (Omvedt 1976; O'Hanlon 1985; Gore 1989). Today, as noted, they account for 45 per cent of the population of Maharashtra.

Some reactionary Brahmans insisted that Maratha claims to Kshatriya status were invalid and relegated them in public pronouncements to the Sudra varna. This denunciation was not forgotten by the Marathas. More moderate Brahmans were eager to obtain support against the British in the freedom struggle. They acknowledged the Kshatriya status of the Marathas and even supported the symbol of Shivaji in the hope of acquiring Maratha allies in the freedom struggle. But even moderate Brahmans continued to extol Brahman social and cultural hegemony and shunt Maratha culture and accomplishments to the background. As a result, Maratha sensibilities were not placated and Marathas were slow to ally themselves with Brahmans in the freedom struggle. Instead Marathas increasingly perceived themselves to be confronted by a Brahman conspiracy designed to sustain Brahman political and economic power and block Maratha ascendancy.

Still, by the 1930s Brahman and Maratha leaders had struck an uneasy alliance in the freedom struggle and they sustained this relationship until independence in 1947. By that time a Maratha *nouveau-riche* was using sugar co-ops to develop an economic foundation in the countryside and build a base of political power. Maratha consciousness had been awakened and they were poised to oppose Brahman's cultural hegemony and political economic domination (Baviskar 1980; Cashman 1975; Kumar 1968).

Gradually the caste contradictions that evoked the conflict between Marathas and Brahmans were resolved in favour of the Marathas. Throughout the 1950s and 1960s Maratha economic and political power increased dramatically. Brahman influence declined accordingly. In 1957 Marathas took control of the government and effectively replaced Brahmans politically in the region that in 1960 became the state of Maharashtra. Marathas now dominate and control the region's economic and political institutions (Lele 1981). Schools and colleges established and supported by Marathas mushroomed in the countryside. They provided important social structures through which Marathas expanded their opportunities and influence (Rosenthal 1977; Zelliot 1982).

Poona University's city colleges and the postgraduate campus are the last bastions of concentrated Brahman hegemony in the state of Maharashtra. Many Brahmans perceive their status to be threatened, not only by the university's affiliated Maratha colleges, but by other universities that Marathas have established recently in the state, such as Shivaji University. Brahmans have responded to these events by proclaiming an increased Hindu chauvinism and identifying with ultraconservative Brahman, or Hindu fundamentalist political associations, such as the RSS (Contursi 1989).

This historical sketch reveals several points that are the basis for conflict in Poona University. Brahman and non-Brahman antagonism in the region is ancient. Marathas believe that Brahmans have impeded their social and economic development. This is an especially bitter complaint, given the discrepancy in size between Brahman and Maratha populations. Many Brahmans still deny the Kshatriya status of the Maratha. They complain that Marathas were not active in the freedom struggle. And they resent the political clout that has permitted Marathas to replace Brahmans in all institutional contexts in Maharashtra, except Poona University.

Historical Consequences

The university's contradictions, especially that of caste, fostered a near paranoia that personnel of opposing castes were conspiring to reduce the influence of others in the university.

Indeed, each can point to circumstances that confirm this perception. On the postgraduate campus non-Brahmans and Brahmans alike remember the long years when Pune Brahmans in the city colleges controlled university government. They remember this as a time when promotions came slowly, if at all, to teachers on the postgraduate campus and the campus suffered from monetary neglect. They believe that given the opportunity, city college Brahmans will reassert their domination. Similarly, Maratha college managements are reluctant to hire Brahmans in general. They believe they will create problems by attempting to reassert their influence and cultural hegemony.

On the postgraduate campus some Brahman teachers complain that Maratha students accuse them of grading them unfairly. The investment of a Maratha Vice-Chancellor in 1978 kindled Brahman fears of the consequences of a Maratha arrogation of university govern-ment. Brahmans complained that "the Marathas" evicted many Brahmans from positions of authority in the university, such as department heads, and replaced them with Marathas, and that they promoted Maratha and non-Brahman teachers rapidly and without merit. They warned that the ascendancy of Marathas would lead to a decline in the quality of postgraduate education.

There is a considerable lore in the university regarding the perception each caste has of others. Local non-Chitpavan Brahmans and non-Brahmans will tell you that Chitpavan Brahmans are notoriously frugal, even cheap. As one non-Brahman teacher described and others corroborated at a social function, it would be characteristic of a Chitpavan not to offer a visitor a glass of water after s/he walked across town to deliver a message when the temperature is 40^{0}C (104^{0}F). In addition, Chitpavans are thought to be conspiratorial, untrustworthy, phlegmatic, and inbred. This latter trait, people assert, is shown by their distinctive phenotype, marked especially by their tendency for blue eyes and a fair complexion.

Chitpavan or Pune Brahmans depict local non-Chitpavan Brahmans as ritually lower in caste, "fish-eaters" as one Chitpavan described them. They also are chided for their rural origins and their role as rural priests, accused of practicing an aberrant Hinduism that is tainted with rural mythology and local deities.

Chitpavan Brahmans also think of Marathas as fairly unattractive, dark, short and stocky. Like rural Brahmans, they are thought to be bumpkins. In addition Marathas are described as peasant in mentality, irredeemably backward and bound to lower the standards of higher education should they come to dominate the university.

Members of each caste delight when a member of the other is implicated in some scandal. It reconfirms Brahman beliefs that Marathas are incompetent and untrustworthy. Equally confirmed are Maratha beliefs that Brahmans are devious, sly, tend to cabals to recapture and retain their power and influence at any cost. The history of the university, especially since 1974, is marked by charges and countercharges by agents of each caste of conspiracy. Each also denigrates at every opportunity the other's status and image. Yet, because overt caste discrimination is evident only occasionally in the fights in the university, it is easy to deny an underlying caste antagonism as a source of the conflict. But the ongoing conflict in the university suggests a dialectic contradiction rooted in these ancient caste antagonisms.

Caste conflicts are not uncommon in India. But in no other region in India did such a small Brahman minority, never more than 5 per cent of the total population, come to assume over the course of 300 years such political and economic dominance and cultural hegemony (Omvedt 1976; O'Hanlon 1985; Gokhale 1988; Gore 1989). The conflict in Poona University is very much a product of this age-old antagonism. The political conflict in the university over the last 40 years was ignited by conscious and unconscious attempts of different leaders to resolve contradictions in the university's caste, institutional and regional alignments.

See Appendix, Episode One: The Maratha-Brahman difference is never far beneath the surface of the university's politics. Shivaji and the Maratha wars are history. But, as Episode One shows, they can be revived for contemporary political purposes.

Notes

1. The University Act of 1994 was promulgated shortly before I arrived. No one knew its implications for university government, and it is not important to this work.
2. Figure 1 shows all the boards and authorities that comprise the structure of the university's government. The following discussion, however, considers only those entities that are critical to the university's politics.
3. Individuals aspire to the office of Vice-Chancellor for a variety of reasons, not the least of which is the power a strong Vice-Chancellor can impose on university policies. But the office also carries attractive perquisites: a car and driver, a comfortable house with servants and attendants, a large salary, travel within India and abroad, and status. A Vice-Chancellor receives considerable deference, is referred to as "Sir," and at university functions people stand when he enters the room.
4. In the varna hierarchy, the Kshatriya varna (warriors and kings) is second to the Brahmans (priests). Vaishayas (merchants) and Sudras (farmers) follow third and fourth, respectively. Traditionally the Kshatriyas have provided the kings and warriors in Hindu society.

III

Chapter

Leaders: Profiles and Projects

Introduction

When faculty members on the postgraduate campus talk in their leisure moments they cover the usual academic prattle about students, colleagues, world affairs, cricket and the like. But, eventually some comment will be made about some aspect of the university's politics. Concern and interest in the university's politics are never much below the surface. The practices of the university's political leaders – they are all well known – are a major topic of these discussions.

Leaders are an essential ingredient of politics. Axiomatically there can be no politics without them. Effective leaders, and this includes those in the university, are characterized by certain nearly universal attributes which, to some extent, vary culturally. For example, some political communities expect their leaders to be bombastic and aggressive. Others may expect them to be unassuming and deferential. But a leader who is mute is not leading at all and will last no longer than one who is all talk and no action. The profile of a successful leader is likely to manifest the following basic traits (Kurtz 2001).

Leaders must be *doers.* They must make things happen for their constituencies. Those who do not lose support quickly. *Visibility* is important. When leaders cause something to happen they must take credit for it if they wish to continue to establish their authority and build power. Negative outcomes can be costly. But there are hedges leaders may develop to reduce them. *Charisma* is one. Of course, not every leader can be charismatic – none of the university's leaders was. And one person's charismatic inspiration is another person's demagogic despot. Charisma also relies on more than leaders' personalities and appearances on *rhetoric*. Leaders must be *talkers*, even where they are expected to be quiet and deferential, for their rhetorical skills are important to their recognition, status, and effectiveness when events require them. *Confidence* is essential for leaders' to build and retain power. Confident leaders will accomplish more than those who are not. *Wisdom, perspicacity and insightfulness* help them to be aware of the total political field and environment within which they operate. *Ambiguity* can disturb followers and cost support. On the other hand, a certain amount of skillfully manipulated ambiguity enhances leader's mystique, keeps opponents off balance, and allows leaders greater latitude of action in the constraints that regulate their practices, such as a constitution, university act, or value structure to which their constituents expect them to conform. Still, *decisiveness* in their actions enriches their status and image and may help constituents forgive them when something goes wrong. Finally, leaders by necessity must be *paranoid*. Any leader who is not is likely to be insane at worst and ineffective at least. Every leader knows that other leaders of equal ability are waiting in the wings of any political structure itching to show that they can do the job better.

Motivations for the actions of leaders who were important to the politics of Poona University derive in part from their personal ambitions in each of the linguistic regions that comprised the Bombay presidences and, in part, from the issues they confronted. But the peculiar strategies by which these leaders pursued their politics – for example, power building through alliance formation – were constructed on the basis of the contradictions in caste, institution and region that permeated the university. Interplay between leaders' strategies and how these contradictions helped to formulate them impelled a history of political conflict that began when the university was first conceived in 1924. The fights became a physical reality when Poona University's first Vice-Chancellor assumed office in 1948 and continued until he was replaced in 1956. This was the period during which agents first attempted to define the purpose of the university.

From 1956 until about 1970 the university enjoyed a period of stasis and relative political calm. During these 15 years university business went on as usual according to the stipulations of the 1948 Act and the power it placed in the hands of city college personnel who comprised university government. The social relations of Vice-Chancellors and their Executive Councils, city college people for the most part, were compatible and their political goals were isomorphic. They strove to develop the excellence of the university by enhancing the programs and facilities of the city colleges. It was not until the late 1960s that leaders began to emerge with projects aimed purposefully at controlling university government.

Throughout these years the postgraduate campus continued to develop, albeit slowly. By the late 1960s teachers on the campus were unhappy with their subordinate status vis-à-vis the city colleges. As the number of postgraduate departments grew their teachers wanted more influence in university government. They had natural allies in the rural Maratha colleges. They also were increasing in number and their personnel wanted more voice in university government.

By the early 1970s everyone in the university knew that a

new university act was imminent, and agents in the rural colleges and on the postgraduate campus were preparing to enter the university's political arenas. The first step they took in this direction was to lobby state politicians to draw up a university act that was sensitive to their goals. In 1974 a new university act superseded the obsolete 1948 University Act. It allowed these agents to compete with agents from the city colleges for positions of power and influence in university government. It also imparted a momentum to the contradictions in caste, institution and region that evoked conflict among political leaders for control of university government that continues today.

The 1974 Act provided considerable clout to teachers on the postgraduate campus and in the rural colleges. But theirs was not an equal relationship. Strong leaders emerged on the campus but not in the rural colleges. Instead, rural college personnel provided a base of power and support for the strategies and tactics that campus leaders would bring to their fights with the city colleges. Before exploring the history of this conflict in the next chapter, it is instructive to introduce the university's political leaders and agents and the projects by which they tried to assert their interests at the expense of competitors.

In the following sections Vice-Chancellors, Executive Councils, and members of the College Teacher's Union were not usually political leaders. They represent political agents. Of these agents only Vice-Chancellors had the opportunity to become political leaders. Most either chose not to or were not able to do so. Some that tried found their efforts precluded by circumstances. There were three exceptions to this. They included the university's first Vice-Chancellor and the last two who occupied the office during this research project. They are subjects of Chapters 7 and 8, respectively. On the other hand, the Gang and the Clique did develop strong leaders. And the Professor, who eventually aligned with the Clique, was the most powerful leader of all.

Leaders and Agents

Vice-Chancellors and Executive Councils

For much of the university's history any aspirations for leadership by Vice-Chancellors and the personnel that constituted their Executive Councils were effectively curtailed by the prescribed periods of time during which they could hold their office and the definitions of the duties of those offices. However, at the time of this research Vice-Chancellors had exceptional power because they could claim access to powers that normally were the prerogative of the Registrar's office. The Registrar is responsible for matters related to university finance, administration and exams. Between 1975 and 1989, a period of extreme political manipulations, the university appointed only acting Registrars, and they were unwilling to get deeply involved in the university's politics. Most Vice-Chancellors chose not to abuse these extra powers. However, the VC (refer to Chapter 3 and again Chapter 7) took advantage of all the sources of power available to him to exercise his project.

Vice-Chancellors were expected to serve a three-year term. For various reasons some served less. Most Vice-Chancellors have not tried to be leaders. This was especially true between 1956 and 1978. However the three-year stipulation for holding office appears to be changing. Four men served as Vice-Chancellors for more than three years. This includes the first Vice-Chancellor (1948-1956). Since then, except for a brief hiatus in 1989, the last three men who occupied the office were elected to two consecutive three-year terms each. These include the first and only Maratha Vice-Chancellor (1978-1984), the VC of Chapter 6, who served only five years (1984-1989), and the Aspirant (1989-1995).

Except for the eight years the first Vice-Chancellor held office, until 1974 Vice-Chancellors and Executive Councillors worked together compatibly. This was the period when the city colleges dominated university government. After 1974, Executive Councillors from the city college usually provided support for the goals of leaders either of the Gang or the Clique. Most often leaders of these teams and their allies held seats on Executive Councils and manipulated their offices and the power vested in them to try to attain their goals. After 1974, Executive Council meetings were politically charged hotbeds. Those Vice-Chancellors who tried to be leaders and challenge their Executive Councils, such as the university's first Vice-Chancellor and the VC (refer to Chapter 3) met formidable resistance.

As noted, in Indian universities Vice-Chancellors are effective to the extent they have a good working relationship with their Executive Councils. Considering that Poona University acquired its first Vice-Chancellor and Executive Council in 1949, the years of greatest compatibility between these authorities were between 1956-1974 when city colleges dominated university government and personnel from the postgraduate campus were excluded. During the years when the Clique dominated university government, 1978-1995, relations between Vice-Chancellor and Executive Councils were stormy because Executive Councils always contained personnel and factions that were antagonistic towards each other. This was largely because these two authorities embodied the university's contradictions in caste, institution and region and the disparate goals sought by the incumbents who represented these contradictions. An overview of some of the practices of Vice-Chancellors and Executive Councils is instructive.

As noted also, Poona University's first Vice-Chancellor, Dr Jayakar, was a CKP, a caste which, recall, has a reputation of being antagonistic to Brahmans. He fought hard from 1924, when Poona University was only an idea, for the creation of the university. He was instrumental in acquiring the estate which the university occupies on a long-term lease from the state of Maharashtra. As Vice-Chancellor for eight years (1948-1956) he directed the initial development of departments on the postgraduate campus. He was forced, however, to work with Executive Councils comprising college personnel, and they strongly opposed his vision of a university dominated by the postgraduate campus. The issues and conflicts of this stormy period are the topic of Chapter 4.

The second Vice-Chancellor, Dr Paranjpye (1956-1959), also was involved in the discussions regarding the establishment of the university in 1924. He was a Pune Brahman and opposed from the first the idea of a strong postgraduate campus. Like all subsequent Vice-Chancellors until 1978, he believed that the university would achieve greatness by promoting the interests of Pune's most prestigious colleges.

From the election of the second Vice-Chancellor in 1956 to 1970 each Vice-Chancellor had an excellent working relationship with his Executive Council which, largely, was composed of representatives of the city colleges. They made sure that a large portion of the resources and gifts that were directed to the postgraduate campus by donation and government grants found their way into the city colleges. One constituent city college, for example, acquired a department of economics that was supposed to be located originally on the postgraduate campus. A separate department of economics was established on the campus only in 1987.

Until 1970 each Vice-Chancellor was a respected member of Indian society and eminently qualified to hold the position. Each also served in an honorary capacity and was appointed without salary. Until the mid-late 1960s the position did not require their attention full time and they continued to pursue their professional careers. By the late 1960s the university was growing more rapidly and its administration required full time attention. To compensate for this, state government amended the 1948 Act to allow Vice-Chancellors to be elected and salaried. Remuneration for the job attracted people in the elections in 1970 who lacked the stature and quality of their predecessors. The Vice-Chancellor and Executive Council who were elected in 1970 became involved in the first factional conflict in the university since Jayakar. Self-indulgence and anarchy prevailed to such an extent that in 1972 the state government and Chancellor demanded the resignation of the Vice-Chancellor, dissolved the Executive Council, and replaced them with a caretaker government composed of government appointees from the city colleges.

Between 1972 and 1978 the sharply different projects associated with the Gang and the Clique crystallized and birthed the conflict over who would control university government. In general, after 1974 Vice-Chancellors increasingly were subject to strong Executive Councils comprising members of these teams. In 1978 the Clique effectively destroyed the power of the CC Leader and Gang. From 1978 to 1984 the Clique dominated the Executive Council and worked compatibly with a Vice-Chancellor of its own choosing. In 1984 the VC (refer to Chapter 6) entered the arena. By 1987 he was totally opposed to the Clique and the Executive Council which its members controlled. This caused a new level of conflict to erupt. In 1987 agents from political parties became part of the university's political field for the first time. This restructured the political field and resources available to it. In 1989 the Aspirant assumed the office of Vice-Chancellor. He was the last member of the original Clique that was the focus of much of this research. His two terms as Vice-Chancellor were fraught by conflict between him and his supporters in the Clique and others, in particular the Brahman lobby, who opposed him.

The College Teachers' Union

Between 1949 and 1974 several Brahman teachers' associations played an important role in university government. They developed in rural colleges in response to grievances teachers had with the policies of college management. Throughout the 1950s and 1960s the growth of rural colleges was slow and the associations responded reasonably well to these grievances. But the growth of rural colleges in the late 1960s and 1970s exacerbated problems between teachers and college managements. Ironically, the associations lost their potential to become a force in university politics in 1974 at just about the same time they merged and were recognized formally by charter as a teachers' union. Very simply, they failed to take advantage of the provisions for power building that the 1974 Act provided.

By 1974, when the College Teachers' Union obtained its charter, teachers' working conditions in rural colleges in particular had deteriorated badly. Teachers lacked job security. Managements expected them to work on an ad hoc, will-call basis, and they were subject to dismissal without cause. Workloads and salaries often depended on the teacher's caste or kin relationship to managements. Pay periods were irregular, and salaries were subject to special withholdings which managements used for a variety of purposes, such as to support a political campaign, help college construction costs, or to honor some important person on some special occasion, such as a politician on his birthday. City college managements contended that the problems were restricted to rural colleges. But a committee established by the state government in 1975 to investigate grievances found the same problems in the city colleges, but less numerous. The union announced that its three major goals were to provide teachers with security in service, a standardized pay schedule and a uniform work load. The union's leadership articulated a vision of a university with a tradition of social justice.

In 1975 college teachers brought over 500 cases before the union's grievance committee. For a few years union leaders seriously challenged the credibility of college managements. Union-management strife was not uncommon. Politicians who ran the colleges tried different tactics to quell dissension and agitation, such as offering union leaders bribes or positions in government. Managements were not very successful in these endeavours. And in one important instance a college management badly misplayed its hand.

On this occasion a union leader managed to tape record an egregious example of management corruption. He intended to take it to a hearing convened by the state government to inquire into union-management problems in the colleges. When the management discovered this it sent some thugs to retrieve the tape. The thugs failed and the tape helped the state government force college managements to change some of their more egregious anti-labour practices.

The union's influence waned for several reasons. As university government adjusted to the growth of the university it was able to rectify many of the grievances that the union had handled. The union lost support as Marathas, who had a natural suspicion of Brahmans, replaced them gradually as teachers in the rural colleges. It lost a lot of credibility in the rural colleges when, in 1974, it moved its headquarters to Pune. Marathas identified Pune, rightly so, as the seat of Brahman power and influence and suspected the union of collusion with Pune Brahmans. Agents on the postgraduate campus also used their control of patronage to provide sufficient largesse to selected supporters to establish a new power base that undercut the union's support dramatically.

Union leaders admit today that their goals were shortsighted. By the time they recognized the potential of the 1974 Act for power building and putting their people in university government offices the union was discredited. Today the union is a minor player in university affairs. It lacks purpose and any long-term strategies to help teachers. Factional fighting among its leadership has further reduced its effectiveness. In general it does very little to improve education.

The City College (CC) Leader and the Gang

The CC Leader, a Deshasta Brahman or, as he said, "a fish-eating sort of Brahman," that is, as noted earlier, one who is ritually lower in caste and comes from a rural area of Maharashtra. He did his postgraduate work in botany at Fergusson College. His status as a rural Brahman studying in Pune elicited some of the prejudices that prevailed at that time. He was ridiculed less for his caste than his rural background. He claimed that this influenced the kind of politics he practiced later. He was the first university politician to seek support from rural Brahman colleges.

By age 25, the CC Leader had earned a M Sc in botany, written his first of several textbooks and became head of the

Botany Department at Fergusson College. He obtained his Ph D in botany from Poona University in 1969. These accomplishments made him more than a little arrogant.

In the mid-1960s, when teachers on the postgraduate campus were beginning to chafe at the city college control of the university, the CC Leader began to develop a project to insure the interests of the city colleges in the university. He was outspoken about his utter disdain for the postgraduate campus. He blamed its teachers for what he perceived to be a decline in morality and justice in Poona University. He claimed that his project would rectify this condition and restore the university's pedagogical purpose and moral direction. Teachers on the postgraduate campus interpreted this, rightly so, to mean that he was going to work to maintain the campus's subordinate status to the city colleges. In his ideal vision of the university, there would be no postgraduate campus. Poona University would be a degree granting institution and all pedagogical pursuits would transpire in the city colleges. The ultimate goal of his project was to become Vice-Chancellor of Poona University.

When the CC Leader began his political career in the mid-1960s he studied the 1948 Act seriously. He knew that it was important to understand the mechanics of its provisions to compete successfully for higher offices in university government. To build support he also used an uncommon strategy at the time. He visited city college teachers in their homes and listened to their grievances. He promised that he would bring their problems to the attention of college management and seek relief on their behalf.

Simultaneously, he worked to obtain support from managements in rural Brahman colleges. He promised to protect them against the self-serving interests of the city colleges and the increasing number of rural Maratha colleges. Representatives of management comprised a voting bloc in university authorities and he was the first leader to exploit this potential in the rural colleges. Brahman managements also were able to exert pressure on teachers to support him. Finally he promised Brahman teachers in rural Maratha colleges that he would work for their interests and protect them from the exploitation of Maratha management.

As a result of these strategies he built an independent bloc of voting support among city college teachers, managements in rural Brahman colleges and Brahman teachers in rural Maratha colleges. Out of these constituencies he forged a coalition of loyal supporters and benefactors that became identified on the postgraduate campus as the Gang. The core membership of the Gang did not constitute a large team. It included a few Brahmans who managed rural Brahman colleges, a few Brahman teachers, and a couple of influential persons in state government. As well as the voting bloc that supported the CC Leader, these individuals brought with them additional supporters on whose votes he could rely. The Gang dominated university government without opposition through their hold on the Executive Council and other university authorities from about 1965 to 1974.

As his power and influence grew the CC Leader ran successfully for seats on various university authorities. He won them largely by defeating Pune Brahmans who still held him in contempt as a rural bumpkin. At the time most people in the university thought that it was impossible for a rural Brahman to accomplish this. But by 1970 he was on the Senate as teachers' representative, the Board of Studies as a department head, and the Academic Council as a result of being nominated by his supporters on the Board of Studies. From these positions he was able to succeed in his project of improving, at least nominally, the lot of city college teachers and the Brahman managements and teachers of some rural colleges who supported him. He enhanced his position with college managements when, in the early 1970s, he established and became head of Symbiosis College in Pune. Although at the time he did not anticipate losing his political clout, he did think of the college as a fall-back system should his political fortunes wane.

Prior to establishing Symbiosis College the CC Leader financed his election campaigns – travel, printing, food, lodging, and the like for him and his staff – largely with royalties from the textbooks he wrote. As well as insuring his livelihood, Symbiosis College also provided him additional financial resources to compete in the fight for control of university government (recall that he charged high fees to attend). He would need these resources. The passage of the 1974 University Act engaged him in a mortal struggle for control of university government. As events unholded, the leaders and agents that emerged on the postgraduate campus developed projects that responded better to the new environment engendered by the 1974 Act. They hoisted the CC Leader on his own petard.

The Clique and Diffuse Leadership

During the long years of city college domination of Poona University, teachers on the postgraduate campus did their work quietly, buried their frustrations over their situation vis-à-vis the city colleges, socialized together and spoke increasingly of the changes they knew were coming. By 1970 the strains of managing the growing university were apparent. The 1948 Act had been amended to finality and no longer responded to the university's problems. These included, among others, the size and complexity of its governing authorities, pressures from the rural colleges for a larger voice in university government and economic distress related to increased deficits due to increased expenses and reductions in state support.

With a new Act imminent, teachers and department heads on the postgraduate campus formed a coalition. Depending on the time, it comprised 15 to 20 Pune, Maharashtra, and outsider Brahmans, CKPs and non-Brahmans. They became the Clique. Built on the frustrations of the previous 18 years the Clique began to develop strategies to abolish city college domination of the university. Despite its diverse caste and regional backgrounds, the Clique had considerable support on campus in its goal of displacing the dominance of the city colleges. Resistance to it would develop later.

The leadership of the Clique was more diffuse than the Gang's. Still, the campus leader, a Chitpavan Brahman and professor of physics, and the Aspirant, a CKP and professor of geography, predominated. In addition, they allowed subordinates and lesser leaders' considerable freedom to act as long as their actions benefited the Clique. Much of the day-to-day work that was important to the development of the Clique's power was the result of these individual's practices.

The Campus Leader, like other Pune Brahmans in the Clique, was dedicated to the postgraduate campus. He was aggressive, ambitious, outspoken and often, to the chagrin of the Clique, acted impulsively, without consulting its other leaders and supporters. He came from a moneyed background, was well-educated and adept at convincing others of his scholarship, creativity, and ability to get things done (see Appendix, Episode Five). He travelled extensively. After a visit to American universities he admired the aggressive and independent behaviour of their faculties. Many teachers on campus, even members of the Clique, felt that he emulated that behaviour too much for the Indian context in which he operated. He desperately wanted to become Vice-Chancellor. In a campus joke that addressed his obsession to be Vice-Chancellor, someone asks him to sign a document. "Not now," he says, "I'll take care of it when I'm VC." This was not to be. The Gang was able to frustrate his bid for the office of Vice-Chancellor. And despite his status as a leader of the Clique, he could not command enough support on campus to win a seat on the Executive Council. Had he become Vice-Chancellor, he had a grandiose vision for a decentralized university. He contended that decentralization would serve better pedagogically and socially the disparate needs of the region the university served. In his plan the rural colleges would be disconnected from the university and the city colleges would be utterly subordinate to the postgraduate campus.

The Aspirant, a CKP, was another leader of the Clique. He was supported especially by its Maratha and outsider Brahman members. I call him the Aspirant because of his quiet aspiration, despite his denials, to become Vice-Chancellor. He finally succeeded to the office of Vice-Chancellor in 1989.

The Aspirant was appointed as a lecturer in geography in 1957. He received no promotion until 1979, shortly after he finished his PhD. Then, during the first term of the Maratha Vice-Chancellor, also a member of the Clique and protégé of the Campus Leader, he moved from Lecturer to Reader to Professor and Head of the Geography Department and powerful positions in university government. He often worked privately behind the scenes to attain his goals. He spent much time either resolving problems created by the Campus Leader, or trying to hold his aggressive nature in check. He was a skilled parliamentarian and shrewd administrator. He also had a reputation as a fixer of problems of uncommon ability. Mainly he extended his assistance to those in the university who had problems with the Gang and city college Brahmans (see Appendix, Episode Three) and leaders of the Clique (see Appendix, Episode Two). It proved to be a good strategy for himself and the Clique. Though he alienated many people, a large part of his support as well as support for the Clique came as a result of his activities and the quiet, persevering support of his friends. Both he and the Campus Leader were known for their generosity to their friends and uncompromising callousness towards their enemies. He shared the vision of the university that was announced by its first Vice-Chancellor, Dr M. R. Jayakar, also, recall, a CKP. In this vision Poona University would be the finest university in India, the "Oxford of the East" that Jayakar had envisioned.

The Professor deserves special attention. The support the Clique had on the postgraduate campus was not sufficient to ensure the defeat of the Gang. To accomplish this, the Clique had to obtain broader support in the rural colleges, for their influence in university government increased greatly after 1974. To gain this support they formed an alliance with the Professor, as some of his friends called him. His enemies, who were many, referred to him in less honorific terms, perhaps the least invidious of which was the "Godfather." It was not an inappropriate title.

Many people thought that the Professor was an original member of the Clique. In fact, he merged with it only around 1981, during the term of the university's first Maratha Vice-Chancellor. By this time his support base in the rural colleges was unassailable. Still, in many rural colleges he is not identified as a member of the Clique. Instead, his rural college supporters perceive him to be a singular force in university government. Indeed from about 1982 to 1989 he was the most powerful and influential person in the university. He argued that the teaching on the postgraduate campus should be dedicated to vocational training. This to him was a way to rectify the unemployment problems in Maharshtra and India at large. His plan would make the postgraduate campus and the rural colleges more equal and sidetrack the city colleges. Of course, such an arrangement also would permit him to sustain the power base he had in the rural colleges without threats either from the city colleges or the postgraduate campus.

The Professor, a Pune Brahman, came from a humble background. He conformed to the dietary proscriptions of the Brahman learna. He was a strict vegetarian, abstained from tea and alcohol, was enthusiastic about sports in which he excelled as a young man, and maintained a humble life-style. He earned his B.A. degree in statistics and economics in 1962. Even before that, in the mid-1950s, he taught in a rural college. After that he also taught in Fergusson College where his students, the Aspirant and Maratha Vice-Chancellor, remember him as a good and dedicated teacher. In the early 1970s the Professor obtained a MSc degree in economics as an external student in a postgraduate program in a city college. He was a member of the college's managing board. In 1975 he enrolled for his PhD in the same college. His focus of study was the economics of energy resources. He expected to receive it in 1986 or 1987. He did not.

He is very capable of peppering his speech with quotes from Shakespeare, John Donne and other English poets, and drawing parallels between events in India's history and the West. Despite this and his obvious eclectic knowledge, he is not a scholar and no longer teaches. The CC Leader was appalled that I referred to him as a Professor. "How could you call that man a Professor?" he protested. Like other members of the Clique, such as the Aspirant, the Professor is a fixer, but perhaps better at it.

In 1985 the Professor earned his living from four sources. He ran a private coaching school to help students pass examinations. He operated a vocational institute in Pune that provided students with some practical vocational training. He also managed a printing press in Pune from which he did much of the university printing, but not without complaint, as we shall see. A less secure source of income came from a rural science college he opened in 1969 in Lonavala, a hill station in the Ghats between Mumbai (Bombay) and Pune. At this point his problems began with the teacher's union and the Gang.

The educational minister who supported the CC Leader and served on the managing board of Symbiosis College wanted control of the Professor's college. He and the CC Leader engaged the union and accused the Professor of unfair labour practices, embezzlement, and mismanagement. Litigation around these issues has persisted over the years since and generated the deep and mutual resentment between the CC Leader and Professor. Although some students have enrolled occasionally in the college and some instruction has taken place, it is closed most of the time.

Many others, especially his detractors, attribute to him a fifth source of income: graft. Some say that graft has made him quite wealthy. They argue that his humble lifestyle is sham to cover his wealth. Others argue that if it is real it is because of the great amount of money he spends to cover the litigation in which he seems to be involved constantly and the travelling and campaigning he must do to retain his powerful support in the rural colleges.

The Professor entered university politics first in 1959. At

that time he ran for the Senate as a representative of the registered graduates. Since then, with only brief interruption between 1972 and 1974 when the Chancellor suspended the Executive Council on which he had a seat, he has served without interruption on various university authorities. His project involved establishing a base of support in the rural colleges to provide a stepping stone to higher office and influence for him and his allies. This strategy was undertaken with the blessing of the Clique.

Sometime around 1975 or 1976 the Professor and Campus Leader agreed to divide spheres of power. They agreed that the Clique would organize support on the postgraduate campus and that it would not intrude into the Professor's efforts to develop a support base in the rural colleges. By that time the Professor and the Cliques leaders had read and mastered the potential of the 1974 Act for acquiring power and they were well prepared to compete in the university's political arenas. As noted, their major goal was the eradication of the Gang. Although the Professor was not a formal member of the Clique at this time, his help was important, but not decisive as we shall see, in the defeat of the Gang in 1978. But after that his power and influence in university government grew considerably.

In the rural colleges the Professor's political organization cut across management, teachers, administrators and students. He was skillful in manipulating them to his ends. He managed this organization so that the interests of one category did not infringe on the interests of the others and yet served his ends effectively by negating the influence of his competitors, such as the Gang, the college teachers' union and a few principals in the rural colleges who did not support him (see Appendix, Episode Two). He did this by dispensing patronage and largesse, controlling the university's authorities, and influencing university appointments. Since college managements, principals, teachers, department heads, and registered graduate students (whom he also represented) each represented a voting constituency in university government, his control of the university by 1986 was quite thorough.

By 1985, with the help of these supporters and his alliance with the Clique, he was on the Senate, was dean of the Natural and Physical Sciences, the highest ranking Dean in the university, and held a seat on the Executive Council which he and his followers dominated. He was also able to place his friends and trusted allies in several critical university positions (his wife was Dean of Education). Through these and his alliance with the Clique, frequently an uneasy relationship as we shall see, he directed the affairs of the university regarding appointments, promotions, program development, allocations of funds, trips overseas and the like.

The Professor's surfeit of enemies on the postgraduate campus and in the city colleges perceive him to be an opportunist who successfully deluded his supporters and is corrupt beyond redemption. He is reported to charge 20 rupees for his signature on anything not directly related to university business. The Dalits who operate the university printing press on campus complain that he filtered most of the university printing work to his printing business in the city. He takes some pleasure in his reputation of being rude, coarse, unscrupulous and loud. He has a reputation for abusing his opponents in meetings and using street tactics that most academicians eschew. They openly proclaim that he bought his masters degree, that he is buying his PhD, and that he has absolutely no qualifications as a scholar.

Still, they acknowledge that his success is due to his

political skills and his singular dedication to helping his friends and those who support him. His loyalty is legendary. Many begrudgingly admire his political acumen. His opponents can expect a no-holds barred fight when they oppose him. If they best him they know that they will be subject to mellifluous overtures to join him and work together for the betterment of higher education (see Appendix, Episode Two). Most do not. But some do. Many wonder why he restricts his political skills to the university.

The Professor's supporters argue that he is dedicated to the betterment of the university; it is not clear to what extent they share his vision of the postgraduate campus as a vocational institution. But even among them there is some dismay regarding his vision of higher education. He is blatantly contemptuous of the vast majority of teachers on the postgraduate campus and in the city colleges. He contends that they are elitist and have an ivory tower mentality that results in training students for non-existent jobs to enhance their own status and prestige. He complains that postgraduate teachers do nothing to improve either the educational climate of the campus or its physical appearance. "They wont even plant a tree to make the campus more beautiful," he complained shortly after he mobilized some students to plant some shrubbery at various places on campus. At times like these he is adamant about the role of the university in providing students with a practical education that emphasizes vocational training instead of abstract knowledge which, from his point of view, provides little of tangible benefit to the students of India.

Paradoxically, he also expresses concern for the lack of communication between himself and teachers on the postgraduate campus. As Dean of Sciences he adopted the motto, "Fill the gap and feel the difference." By this he meant that the communication gap between him and teachers somehow ought to be bridged. While he laments that he did not establish better communication with the postgraduate teachers, he thinks that it is now too late to do so. His solution to filling the gap and silencing those who, according to him, slander him and sustain strife in the university is to procure the appointment and promotion of his followers. That has been a major thrust of his project.

The Professor often holds court and conducts business on the low stone wall across the street from the old administration building on the postgraduate campus. He is obvious by his booming, rasping voice and the red handkerchief he keeps around his neck under the collar of his shirt. His enemies frequently sneer at his behaviour (he often shouts at people passing by to come before him) and sartorial habits and consider them a crude and ostentatious affectation. He sits there, he told me, because he had no office in the overcrowded administration building and wears the handkerchief to keep his shirt collar clean from sweat so he can wear it an extra day.

The Clique became a force to reckon with in 1974. Its leadership methodically sought support from a wide variety of constituencies on the postgraduate campus. The Campus Leader even worked hard to develop support in the rural colleges. He did this by making presentations and providing the latest ideas and equipment to the physics departments of selected rural colleges. Despite the different visions its leaders had of the university the Clique's primary project was simple: it was devoted passionately to overthrowing the Gang and the CC Leader and disposing of any vestige of city college control of the postgraduate campus.

There was considerable debate on the campus regarding who precisely constituted the Clique. This was because by

1985-1986 the Clique's core membership – those 15 to 20 outsiders, Maharashtra and Pune Brahmans, Marathas, and other non-Brahmans – was not always clearly perceived by others. In addition to the Campus Leader and Aspirant, the Professor rounded out the Clique's diffuse leadership. Each of these men also had two or three other individuals, loyalists, who served him as close lieutenants. Each of these lieutenants also had a few, albeit somewhat fluid, loyal and trusted followers from various caste backgrounds upon whom they made sure the leaders could rely. This constituency made up the core of the Clique. In addition, by 1985-1986 the Clique had the support of about 10 department heads on the postgraduate campus, an ex-Vice-Chancellor, the heads of about six major campus programs, and a great number of teachers – some said at least one in every department – for whom they had either fixed or were fixing things. And the Professor had massive support from Marathas in the rural colleges.

Some have argued that the disparate composition of the Clique denies the argument that caste was a significant factor in university politics. Its composition was not a haphazard agglomeration. It was logical in terms of who it recruited. But it also represented the fault lines along which the caste contradiction was expressed in the university. Some of these individuals did not get along well and obligations to each other varied considerably. But it was their mutual allegiance to the postgraduate campus and utter disdain for the city colleges that held them together. As the institutional contradiction was resolved gradually in favour of the postgraduate campus, caste and regional contradictions assumed a more important role in the conflict, and the reputation and integrity of the Clique suffered.

See Appendix, Episode Two: The machinations of the

university's leaders as they pursue their goals pervade this work. Episode Two shows how these leaders and agents try to manipulate hiring practices to favour candidates of one caste or another – Brahman or Maratha – and the nuisance value these tactics may involve.

IV

Chapter

Early Conflict: Postgraduate Campus and City Colleges (1924-1970)

Introduction

As noted, the idea of creating a university in Pune was first discussed in 1924. The Brahman- non-Brahman division that would dominate the history of conflict in Poona University was symbolized by the castes of the individuals who were involved most deeply in those first discussions (Golay 1974). Dr M. R. Jayakar, a CKP by caste, land, Dr R. P. Paranjpye, a Pune Brahman, would serve as its first two Vice-Chancellors respectively. Dr Jayakar was the leader of the pro-university forces. The Deccan Educational Society and other Pune Brahmans, including Dr Paranjpye, distrusted him because of his vision of the university and his caste's long tradition of anti-Brahman sentiments (Gokhale 1988). They were apprehensive, though not hostile, regarding the idea of a university in Pune.

Even though a few rural Maratha colleges existed at this time and a few more opened after 1924, they were not involved much in discussions regarding the university. But given post-independence expectations regarding the role of higher education in the economic and social development of India, it was only a matter of time before they would become part of the university's dialectic. In Maharashtra it could not be otherwise. The countryside was Maratha, agricultural, and developing. By the 1930s the shift toward Maratha political and economic domination of the countryside was well underway (Sirsikar 1972; Cashman 1975). The region's political economy, caste structure, and creation of a Marathi speaking state in 1960 were instrumental in bringing the rural Maratha colleges into the university's political arenas and the debates regarding the university that began years before.

In 1943 the government of the Bombay Presidency decided to establish a university in the region that would become the state of Maharashtra and recommended Pune as its most desirable location. This was based on the recommendation of a committee that was chaired by Dr Jayakar (Vice-Chancellor, 1948-1956) and included Dr Paranjpye, the second Vice-Chancellor (1956-1959) and another future Vice-Chancellor. Although Jayakar and Paranjpye agreed that a university was desirable, their conception of it differed seriously. Squabbles over its jurisdiction and relationship to the city colleges developed early and increased in volatility.

Jayakar versus Paranjpye

Jayakar was an eminent member of the legal profession and an influential political leader at the local and regional levels. He envisioned a university comparable to Oxford and Cambridge in England and, as noted, thought of Poona University as the "Oxford of the East". In his vision the university would develop around a residential campus with strong postgraduate teaching departments. It would be an elite institution with a wide jurisdiction that affiliated all colleges in that jurisdiction to the postgraduate campus. Its teaching staff would be recruited from among the best scholars in India, and they would dispense a liberal education that was relevant to national as well as local and regional elites.

Paranjpye was a professor and previous Principal of Fergusson College. He envisioned a university with a jurisdiction limited to an area of about two miles radius from Pune. His university would incorporate the city colleges as the university's constituent components. Graduate courses would continue to be taught in the colleges. Postgraduate courses would be taught on the postgraduate campus by a staff recruited from among the most eminent teachers in the colleges. Education would be especially relevant to the region, narrowly defined.

Each point of view had supporters, and debate among organizations, or *mandals*, representing caste, educational and other interests in Pune was intense. One hears little of Paranjpye today. It was Jayakar's vision that the 1948 Act embodied, at least in principle. Practice was another matter.

The conversion of Jayakar's vision into reality was fraught with conflict that embittered him and has persisted since. The major problem he confronted was the stipulation in the 1948 Act that precluded postgraduate campus teachers from serving on the most critical university authority, the Executive Council. As a result, until 1974, the Executive Council was dominated by Pune Brahmans from the city colleges. As its nominal founder and champion, teachers on the postgraduate campus and many others in the university at large revere Jayakar. But those whose sentiments lay with the city colleges, such as the CC Leader and Gang, depict him as a mere forerunner of the Clique.

During the 25 years between 1924 and 1949 the university was only an idea subject to debate. These years provided ample time for those concerned with the university to harden their positions regarding its final structure and organization. Agents in the city colleges who supported the idea of a local university had strong support from the local Brahman community, the Congress Party which Pune Brahmans dominated at the time and powerful and influential Brahman educational societies, such as the Deccan Educational Society (see Appendix, Episodes Three and One). The dedication of the local Brahman community to their colleges presented a persistent problem for Jayakar and his supporters. And the exclusion of postgraduate campus teachers from participation in the university's highest authority insured that the university's government would be dominated by principals, teachers, postgraduate students (alumni), and others dedicated to the city colleges. Their resistance frustrated the implementation of much of Jayakar's vision of the university. It is a credit to his political perseverance that he was able to lay the foundation for strong postgraduate departments.

Jayakar's terms in office were tumultuous. Every action taken by Jayakar and his supporters, even to acquiring the 411 acres (later reduced to 409 acres as we shall see below) of land that the university occupies on a long-term lease from the Government of Maharashtra, met with resistance from the city colleges. In 1955, for example, Fergusson College tried to insure that postgraduate work in geology would be conducted on its campus, even though a building to house geology had been constructed on the postgraduate campus.

But the major issue that consumed Jayakar's eight years in office was a provision in the Act concerned with intermediate and graduate teaching. Until the university was founded the colleges provided the fours years of education that led either to the BA or BSc degree. The first two years of that education comprised the period of intermediate instruction; the last two comprised graduate instruction. Jayakar and his supporters wanted to centralize graduate teaching on the postgraduate campus and restrict the colleges to providing only the first two years of intermediate instruction. This would effectively relegate the colleges to the status of two-year junior colleges. The agents representing the colleges feared that if the university did not permit them to continue to provide graduate teaching, they would become insignificant. City college agents considered the language of the Act on this matter to be sufficiently ambiguous to challenge the centralization of graduate teaching on the postgraduate campus. The Act states that:

> Within the area of Poona, all instruction and training beyond the stage of the intermediate examinations and within the university area shall be postgraduate instruction, teaching and training shall be conducted by the University and shall be imparted by the teachers of the University: Provided that a constituent degree college or a constituent recognized institution shall supplement such teaching by tutorial or other instruction, teaching or training in the manner to be prescribed by the Regulations to be made by the Academic Council (1948 Act, p. 272).

Jayakar and his supporters contended that the Act clearly charged the postgraduate campus ("the University," as the Act refers to it) with responsibility to provide graduate education. The Academic Council and Executive Council, each dominated by city college personnel, supported the colleges' interpretation. They fought to retain graduate teaching and develop postgraduate departments in the colleges and to have college teachers conduct any postgraduate teaching that took place on the postgraduate campus.

Agents on both sides of the issue suggested schemes to comply with this provision of the Act. One adopted by the Executive Council established centres for teaching various subjects in different city colleges. It retained graduate education in the city colleges. But it also required students to move around Pune to comply with graduation requirements and satisfy their interests. It was clumsy and unworkable. No one was happy. Attempts by Jayakar and university authorities to find a solution were riddled with conflict.

Jayakar, of course, opposed the centralization of graduate education and the development of postgraduate departments in the colleges. But city college domination of the university's authorities that decided these matters made it difficult for him. As a result, he sought allies elsewhere. He finally asked the Chancellor to clarify the provisions of the Act regarding this matter. The Chancellor's agreed with him in principle and supported the idea of a centralized university in which all education above the intermediate examinations was provided by the postgraduate campus. But he added the proviso that centralization should be accomplished gradually. This decision did not allay the conflict.

The colleges sought another interpretation from the next Chancellor. He concurred with his predecessor's decision. Nonetheless, Jayakar found himself in a constant fight, and some of his responses were less than judicious. This proved to be unfortunate for future relations between the postgraduate campus and city colleges. The report of one committee that Paranjpye, the second Vice-Chancellor, convened to explore the entire issue concluded that Jayakar should have been less legalistic and more humanistic in his relations with the colleges. But it also admonished the colleges for their intransigence and obstructionist activities.

The issue was resolved in 1958, during Dr Paranjpye's term as Vice-Chancellor. University authorities adjusted the formula that established the number of years required by students to graduate in a way that was favourable to the city colleges. Teachers on the postgraduate campus were not permitted to engage in graduate teaching. It remains the prerogative of the colleges. Nonetheless, the issue persisted over whether the city colleges or the postgraduate campus would dominate higher, postgraduate education.The conflict established precedents that continue to affect the university. During this controversy city college agents openly and repeatedly attacked the postgraduate campus. This resulted in considerable animosity in Pune toward's the campus, and this persists. The practice of using the local press, largely sympathetic to Pune's Brahman community, to make all university matters public in order to drum up support for one position or another also developed at this time, and this persists. The constant exposure of problems between city colleges and the postgraduate campus exacerbated their schism. Agents involved in political fights today continue this tactic. Unfortunately, these practices keep university problems, real and imagined, in the public domain, and detract from the contribution and value of the postgraduate campus to the community.

Dr Jayakar left office a man embittered by the fights and the knowledge that the city colleges would dominate the university through their control of Executive Councils and the Vice-Chancellors office. He did not visit the university again, except in 1958. At that time the newly completed library was named after him. Subsequent Vice-Chancellors worked hard to tilt the balance of resources and influence in favour of the city colleges. Nonetheless postgraduate teaching and research gradually became a small but solid reality on the postgraduate campus.

Subsequent Vice-Chancellors

Each of the six men who served as a Vice-Chancellor between 1956 and 1970 did so in an honorary capacity, without remuneration. Each was a distinguished individual and a Pune Brahman. One was a member of the bar, another was a respected politician. The other four were scholars and held higher degrees either from prominent Indian or European universities. Several had strong political connections to the Congress Party. Two were considered to be Party intellectuals. The actions and decisions of these men show their strong ties and commitments to the city colleges.

At one point a Vice-Chancellor returned two acres of the estate that the postgraduate campus occupies to the state government to enable the construction of an industrial research laboratory. Given the 411 acres that the campus occupied the amount of land ceded to the state government was insignificant. Yet, some people on the postgraduate campus still think of the action as an unjust redistribution of its land. Another attempted to establish an undergraduate science college in the city in opposition to the UGC recommendation. And several continued efforts to increase the involvement of college teachers in postgraduate campus departments and to establish postgraduate centres in city colleges. Some people on the postgraduate campus recall with special bitterness that agents in the city colleges worked with a Vice-Chancellor to thwart a recommendation by the UGC to establish the postgraduate campus as a prestigious National University, similar to Jawaharlal Nehru University and Benares Hindu University. Throughout this period funds from a variety of sources and staff positions allocated to the postgraduate campus found their way to various colleges. Appointments to the postgraduate campus were always difficult (see Appendix, Episode Three).

Nonetheless, this was a period of relative political calm. In effect, the hegemony of city colleges was sufficient to avert serious confrontation with agents on the postgraduate campus. Largely because of these halcyon times the Vice-Chancellors acquired a certain mystique through their selfless dedication to administering the university without remuneration. It is primarily Pune Brahmans and city college agents who venerate these men. Another reality exists from the viewpoint of personnel on the postgraduate campus. They see little benefit to the campus as a result of these administrations. No one speaks ill of them. But postgraduate teachers are quick to point out that the postgraduate campus suffered because of their policies. Regardless, this tranquility was about to be upset by processes that were occurring in the countryside and interior to the university. They were not mutually exclusive.

Rural Development and Maratha Colleges

The ancient rivalry between Brahmans and Marathas extended to almost every sphere of social life and activity in the region (Joshi 1967; Kamat 1980a, 1980b). It intensified after 1930 as the trend toward is Maratha cultural, political and economic domination in the region became stronger. It culminated in 1957. At that time Marathas replaced Brahmans in the government of what would become the state of Maharashtra in 1960 and, for all practical purposes, assumed political and economic dominance in the region.

During the years the government worked to create the state of Maharashtra it attempted to incorporate as many Marathi speakers as possible into its boundaries. These were largely rural peasants. As Brahmans faced their numerical insignificance and waning political and economic power they tried to hold on to what positions of influence they could. Higher education assumed primary importance. But, given the bigger problems related to the creation of Maharashtra that occupied the state's politicians and legislators, Poona University's problems were relatively insignificant. In large part this was because the politicians were overwhelmingly rural Marathas and they were concerned with bringing education to their rural consti-tuencies. They opened two Maratha-based universities in the countryside in 1958 and 1962, respectively, and others later. Maratha politicians also began to establish colleges in their districts. As one informant stated, the politicians' ideas of modernization meant that villages ought to receive a post office, telegraph office, railroad station, and college in that order. From a purely political consideration the college was the most important.

The 13 constituent city colleges and research institutions and 14 affiliated rural colleges, some of the earliest of which were Brahman, that existed in 1949 increased in number gradually until the 1960s. After that rural colleges in particular were established more rapidly. Fifty-seven rural colleges emerged between 1967 and 1972. By the time the 1974 Act was approved another 37 rural colleges, a total of 92, mostly Maratha, were affiliated to the university. By 1974 the 13 constituent city colleges and institutions had increased to 37. The growth of rural colleges was due primarily to the relationship that developed between rural Maratha politicians and cooperatives involved in sugar production.

In 1951 a total of four sugar cooperatives operated in India at large. By 1978, 56 cooperative sugar factories were operating in the state of Maharashtra alone, and 14 others were in various stages of construction (Baviskar 1980). The colleges that were owned and managed by sugar cooperative were established by Maratha politicians who now also dominated the Congress Party.[1] They were quick to see political and economic advantage in the expansion of higher education in the countryside (Rosenthal 1977; Lele 1981; Baviskar 1980).

Maratha universities and colleges were modern instruments and symbols of the re-emergence of Maratha power and influence. But their symbolic importance seemed to have little to do with education. Regardless of politicians rhetoric that extolled the virtues of education in the countryside, the politician's who established the colleges were generally insensitive to the problems of rural education: non-dedicated teachers, caste bias and nepotism in recruiting teachers and students, cheating, inadequate facilities, low salaries and the like. They used the colleges as political resources to gain and hold political offices in the state government.

In rural colleges especially, a teacher's job security, or the quality of the job, often depended on the support she gave to local politicians. National political parties, such as the Congress Party and Bharatiya Janata Party (BJP), each of which is important in Maharashtra politics, also used the colleges as training grounds for party cadres. They actively recruited and supported financially student campaigns for college government and groomed the students for subsequent roles in state and national government. Political parties also may mobilize these students to disrupt academic functions and for non-academic purposes (see Appendix, Episode Six).

University politicians also were becoming aware of the potential rural colleges provided as political resources in university politics. As early as 1956, during the fights over the distribution of intermediate and graduate teaching, the city colleges vented frustration at what they perceived to be more autonomy among the rural colleges regarding program development than they had. This may have been political rhetoric. But by 1966, rural colleges became significant enough in university affairs that the extant Vice-Chancellor admonished the city colleges in his retirement address for ignoring their needs.

By 1970, tensions between rural and city colleges regarding their respective roles in university government were palpable. And by 1974, rural college managements and teachers were anxious for a voice in university government. But there were other motivations for such participation than improvement of rural education.

Participation in university politics provided some teachers and management figures with additional funds that often were significant. Participants in university government are reimbursed for daily and travel expenses when they attend meetings on the postgraduate campus. Much of the participation of teachers, principals, and management figures was always in support of one leader or another, especially the CC Leader and Professor. And these leaders were always generous in their largesse and patronage. Excessive padding of bills and accounts were easily overlooked. And teachers in good standing with leaders could also earn extra money reading examinations. Using these tactics the CC Leader built a base of support among the managements of rural Brahman colleges. In 1974 the Professor was beginning to use these tactics to put together a coalition of Maratha teachers, principals, and management personnel. On the other hand, just as other agents were beginning to enhance their political support in the rural colleges, the Teachers' Union's political influence in university affairs began to wane.

The Teachers' Union

When the Teachers' Union attempted to organize rural college teachers who, in 1949, were largely Brahman, college managements engaged in a classic divide and rule policy to stifle the growth of the union. They created suspicion among Maratha teachers of the union's goals by emphasizing its Brahman composition and support of Brahman teachers. But as economic and political changes gradually created more colleges and more jobs, managements had to become more sensitive to teacher's concerns. By the early 1960s, both Maratha teachers in rural colleges and city college teachers were joining the union.

For a few years in the 1960s and 1970s the union had some success in recruiting members and working on their behalf. These efforts followed traditional union concerns, such as improved working conditions and better pay. But by 1974 other political agents were beginning to develop the potential of the new 1974 Act to out-manoeuvre the union and subsequently overwhelm it as a force in university politics. Several factors accounted for this.

New agents, such as the CC Leader and Professor, were emerging. They were concerned less with teachers' welfare than attaining control of university government. They spoke of justice for teachers. But their projects required political power. That meant they had to seek support selectively to win the fights that were developing in the university. Despite the long tradition of anti-Brahman sentiment in the region, rural Maratha teachers, especially, but also some Maratha managements, found themselves subordinate to Brahman political leaders on the postgraduate campus, such as the Campus Leader and Professor. And city college teachers found themselves subordinate to the Gang and the CC Leader. Recall that the CC Leader was a rural Brahman and his major allies in the Gang were the managements of rural Brahman colleges.

The union supported the 1974 Act because it promised to

democratize university government. It did not anticipate the potential of the Act for power building. The rural Brahmans that directed the union also were naive about the extent of anti-Brahman sentiment in the countryside. In 1974 the union's leadership moved its headquarters to Pune to be close to the seat of emerging power and influence on the postgraduate campus. They did not anticipate that Maratha teachers would interpret this as a move towards Brahman collusion. Maratha rural college managements exploited these suspicions. They continued to warn against Brahman domination of education and to point out that the union hierarchy was Brahman. This move cost the union considerable support.

The development of factional politics in the union further reduced its efficiency. And some of its tactics, such as scheduling strikes during examination periods, provided issues upon which others capitalized. Neither the Gang nor the Clique nor the Professor supported the union, and they were successful in averting strikes.

The Professor was especially antagonistic to the union. They were competing for the same resource – rural Maratha teachers. And the collision of the Professor and union was accelerated when the union helped the CC leader take the Professor to court on charges of corruption and mismanagement of his college in Lonavala in 1972-1974. After 1974 the Professor was increasingly successful in nullifying the union's influence.

The Gang and the Professor: The Beginning

The CC Leader and Gang were unopposed in university government during the 1960s. They dominated the Executive Council and worked compatibly with the Vice-Chancellors of that period. Although the CC Leaders initial support came from city college teachers, he expanded it, although not extensively, among Brahman teachers in the rural college. To insure this support he devoted much of his attention to looking after the welfare of the Gang and his supporters. He did this by encouraging their participation on various university committees and authorities and rewarding them through his largesse and patronage.

For example, he managed to place his friends on the university committee that allocated examination duties to teachers and dispersed the funds to pay them for the service. Of course, he oversaw the distribution of the exam duties and the funds, and he was discriminating in their allocation. He rotated examinations among potential readers and thus spread his largesse among his supporters. He also made sure that university administration, which was lax to begin with, overlooked how his allies who travelled to the postgraduate campus (or elsewhere) to read exams or attend meetings padded their travel and daily allowance expenses. This was especially lucrative for management personnel who were required to make several visits a year to the campus. Knowledgeable sources in university administration claimed that one college principal earned an extra 15,000 rupees in one year in this way. At the time that was equivalent to several months' salary for a college teacher. The CC Leader did not deny this amount when I asked him about it. Today these allowances are far less lucrative.

At the time it did not seem important to him to curry the favour of Maratha teachers and management. Brahmans had always been in control of higher education in the region. He assumed they always would be. Given events and conditions during the 1960s this perspective did not seem shortsighted.

It was.

The CC Leader also looked out for himself. In the 1960s he thought himself to be an indestructible force in university government. Still, he was shrewd enough to know that one's political fortunes can wane. Recall that Symbiosis College was a hedge against that possibility, and he used his influence to establish it. A state minister and the Vice-Chancellor at the time helped him get the land necessary for the college's construction. The university approved the college quickly and it opened in the mid-1970s. As a result, he gained additional influence in university politics as a representative of college management. This enhanced his relationship with Brahman management in rural and urban colleges. The state minister, who is still influential, although now out of office, remains a member of the college's board of directors. The college augmented the power and influence of the CC Leader in university government. But he was beginning to make decisions that would in the long run have unforeseen and negative consequences.

Recall that a major thrust of his rhetoric and project was to seek justice and inject some moral purpose into the affairs of the university. He was irritated by a situation which will be discussed in detail in the next chapter. It concerned changes in the late 1960s regarding procedures by which Vice-Chancellors were appointed. He challenged these procedures. This triggered the events between 1970 and 1972 that caused the state government to dissolve and reappoint a new Vice-Chancellor and Executive Council to govern the university between 1972 and 1974. The 1974 Act was another consequence of these events. Ultimately the new Act caused him to suffer for his hubris and actions.

While the CC Leader was exerting great influence in

university affairs, the Professor was just beginning his university political career. No one remembers anything significant about him during the 1960s. By his own assessment he was a loner in the university's politics and served quietly in the Senate. He first moved into a position of real influence in 1969. At that time he was elected to the Executive Council. But, like the CC Leader, he was caught up in the events that suspended the Executive Council in 1972. For a couple of years his role in university government was severely curtailed. These events also provided his first encounter with the CC Leader and they became mortal enemies. These events are the topic of the next chapter.

Notes

1. The Congress Party initially was a Brahman-based party with a wide constituency throughout India. It retains much of that constituency. But in Maharashtra, after the creation of the state in 1960, Marathas gradually co-opted the party.

V
Chapter
The Era of the Gang: The 1974 Act and Challenge to the Gang's Hegemony (1970-1978)

Introduction

By 1970 the conflict generated by the contradictions embedded in Poona University was about to enter a new phase. Strong agents, such as the CC Leader and the Gang, were replacing Vice-Chancellors and their Executive Committees as dominant forces in university politics. Teachers on the postgraduate campus were restive. The Campus Leader was emerging as a force to contend with. The political projects, strategies and power plays of these agents began to complement the parliamentary procedures that prevailed previously. Two events were about to unleash latent contradictions that were to propel a splay of conflict that would become integral to the university's political processes. These were the election of the Vice-Chancellor in 1970 and the replacement of the 1948 University Act with the 1974 Act (Golay 1974).

The CC Leader and the Gang, the dominant coalition on the Executive Council, were deeply involved in the process that led to these events. Gradually the political field expanded as other agents saw the possibility of gains to be made as a result of the changes that were overtaking the university. Secondary institutional and regional contra-dictions in the university – rural colleges, city colleges, postgraduate campus – were about to feed into its primary caste contradiction.

1970-1972

As the university developed, the 1948 Act required recurrent amendment to cope with its increasing complexity and problems. The amendment that provided remuneration for the Vice-Chancellor had profound effects. Legislators and university personnel alike thought the salary and related perquisites – car and driver, residence, allowances, servants and prestige – that was approved for the Vice-Chancellor in 1967 would continue to attract outstanding candidates. No one gave much thought to the possibility that the salary might attract individuals of lesser quality, especially since the first Vice-Chancellor who was eligible for the salary in 1967 declined it. But if the salary for the Vice-Chancellor was about to attract individuals of lesser quality to the office, adjustments in the practice by which Vice-Chancellors were selected evoked the baser sensibilities of the candidates for the office in 1970. Even though the 1948 Act prescribed the procedure for selecting and appointing the Vice-Chancellor, in practice another procedure was followed prior to 1970.

According to the 1948 Act, members of the Senate were required to elect the Vice-Chancellor from a slate of three names approved by the Executive Council. The winner was supposed to be appointed formally by the Chancellor. However, prior to 1970 a selection committee appointed by the Executive Council submitted a list of three names directly to the Chancellor. Then, by prearranged agreement, two candidates withdrew and the third, always a distinguished gentleman with the proper credentials, received the appointment. The CC Leader thought this was an unethical and "immoral" practice. Morality loomed large in the CC Leader's values. He used the Gang's political clout to force compliance with the Act in the 1970 election of Vice-Chancellor. For the first time candidates for Vice-Chancellors competed for the support and vote of senators.

In 1970 three men, none of whom had the credentials of the previous Vice-Chancellors, contested hotly for the office. One was an ear, nose and throat surgeon. He had the support of the CC Leader. They were close friends and political allies. The other two were college principals. Each was a member of the Executive Council and had his name submitted to the Senate. This was not illegal according to the Act. But because these practices dispensed with the compilation of a list of candidates by the Executive Council some people felt that is was ethically questionable.

Sharply drawn divisions cleaved along lines of support for each candidate. This was an unforeseen consequence of compliance with the 1948 Act. The surgeon won because the CC Leader successfully engineered his election campaign from his position of power and influence. At this time the CC Leader held seats on the Executive Council, the Senate, Board of Studies and Academic Council. But it was a close race and the outcome was decided in a manner that was unacceptable to the losers.

The election procedure prescribed by the Act was complicated. It was conducted according to a system of proportional representation by means of a single transferable ballot cast by each member of the Senate. Each senator was required to mark a first and second preference on the ballot he submitted. The wisdom of this was revealed when the tally of ballots after the first vote did not provide any candidate with the majority of votes necessary to win. As a result the lowest ranking candidate was eliminated. The votes on his ballots were then transferred to the remaining candidates according to the second preference marked on each ballot. This resulted in a tie. Therefore, as prescribed by the Act, the candidate with the highest number of votes on the first ballot, in this case the surgeon, was proclaimed the winner.

Both losers challenged the procedure. But it was upheld by the Chancellor and, upon subsequent appeals, the state supreme court. Thereafter the losers (who remained on the Executive Council) and their followers disrupted Council meetings. One member of the opposition, a lawyer, referred every issue to a stack of legal tomes he carried to each meeting. This tactic often consumed hours. Shouting matches between the Gang and opponents became commonplace. Meetings frequently dragged on into the night. The conduct of university business became contentious, difficult and plodding.

The fortuitous resolution of this election denied the Vice-Chancellor a legitimate base of support. He also lacked the decorum that previous Vice-Chancellors brought to the office, and his personal conduct reduced his legitimacy even further and exacerbated his problems. He engaged in a variety of indiscretions and gratuitous self-indulgences.

The CC Leader disagreed and tried to disassociate himself from the Vice-Chancellor and his immoral behaviour. Local newspapers had an editorial feast at the Vice-Chancellor's expense. The aura associated with the selflessness and prestige of the university's Vice-Chancellors evaporated, and the CC Leader was embarrassed at his support of the Vice-Chancellor.

By 1972 university business had ground to a halt. The Chancellor was under pressure to rectify the situation. But, since the Vice-Chancellor was well fixed with the Congress

Party, the Chancellor did not want to act precipitously and create even larger problems. Friends of the Vice-Chancellor finally convinced him to resign. At that point the Chancellor also suspended the Executive Council.

For two years, from 1972 to 1974, a Vice-Chancellor and Executive Council appointed by the Chancellor managed the affairs of the university. The Vice-Chancellor was a respected principal from Fergusson College, and the Executive Council was composed primarily of respected principals from city colleges. They got along marvellously and these two years were relatively quite and uneventful (see Appendix, Episode Three, for some of the problems that transpired during this time). This was the calm before the storm, for the state legislature was busy drafting a new university act.

These events strongly influenced the CC Leader's political career, for he was deeply involved. He claims that he was offended by the immorality of the process by which Vice-Chancellors were selected traditionally and that motivated him to initiate the electoral process stipulated by the Act. But he also admitted that by this time he was thinking of contesting for the office of Vice-Chancellor, and given his base of support, an electoral process would be to his advantage.

But the CC Leader also was becoming arrogant. He told me that after the surgeon was elected he "felt like a king maker; the power behind the throne." He said that the sense of power was beginning to go to his head. Still, he did not enjoy total support from city college personnel. In part this was because of his support to the errant Vice-Chancellor, in part because of his hubris and in part because some Pune Brahmans still considered him to be a rural bumpkin. He also held teachers on the postgraduate campus in utter and open disdain and treated them as inferiors. All this would cost him later.

The suspension of the university's government in 1972 was a sobering experience for the CC Leader. As a member of the suspended Executive Council he lost that seat, although he continued to hold his other posts. He remained influential and visible. But it was not an especially auspicious time for him to flaunt his political acumen.

By 1970 other agents, such as the Clique and Professor, were becoming politically active, although neither could challenge the power of the CC Leader and Gang. The Professor, for example, had served in the Senate for many years and had built sufficient support to contest in 1969 for a seat as the Senate's representative on the Council. He won. But since he supported one of the losing candidates for Vice-Chancellorship in 1970 he ran afoul of the Gang. Shortly after the Professor occupied his seat on the Executive Council the Gang discovered a technical flaw in his election that allowed it to remove him from office. Although he retained his seat in the Senate, as the statutes allowed, he retreated to relative obscurity. This was a critical period in the development of his project. During this time he began to build his support in the rural colleges. But the Professor did not forget his treatment by the Gang. And conflict later over his college in Lonavala would exacerbate their rivalry.

The Clique also was beginning to organize at this time. After the elections of 1970 it was common knowledge that a new university act was imminent. People in the university also knew that the Campus Leader would have to be dealt with in any university government that awarded power to postgraduate teachers. He had by this time established a reputation as an aggressive personality who got things done, with the help of the Clique, of course.

The 1974 Act

The imbroglio around 1970-1972 provided the catalyst by which the contradictions in the university gained expression. As noted, the 13 constituent city colleges and institutions and 14 affiliated rural colleges that existed in 1949 increased to 37 and 92, respectively, by 1974. The regional contradiction and its attendant caste and institutional variants had become significant. The rural colleges wanted more voice in university affairs. The 1974 Act was their mechanism of ingress.

The city colleges, postgraduate campus teachers, registrars, registered graduates and a variety of other constituencies in the university made recommendations to the 1974 Act. But it was essentially a creation of the managements and politicians who ran the rural Maratha colleges and it had widespread support among the Maratha legislators that dominated state government that drew up the Act. The 1974 Act as finally constructed was a response to the shift in power relations in the university from Brahmans to Marathas, similar to that which transpired earlier when Marathas replaced Brahmans in state government. In effect, the 1974 Act was a revolt against the control of university government by Pune Brahmans in city colleges. It evoked the institutional and regional contradictions embedded in the university's structure. As a result of the subsequent fights, by 1986 the city colleges were largely isolated from university politics.

In addition to enfranchising previously ignored constituencies in the university, the 1974 Act restructured recruitment procedures to the offices of university government and the structure of that government. Even though the fiasco of the 1970 elections was a singular event, it showed the potential for conflict that the election of a Vice-Chancellor could induce. The 1974 Act retained electoral processes as the means of recruitment to most university offices. But it rejected the idea of an election for the office of Vice-Chancellor. Instead it prescribed a procedure by which the Chancellor appointed a person to the office.

The 1974 Act required individuals and constituencies to submit the name of candidates they were interested in having considered for the office of Vice-Chancellor to a three member committee, each of which was selected, respectively, by the Executive Council, the Academic Council and the Chancellor. The committee then, upon deliberation, selected three individuals from that pool and submitted this slate to the Chancellor. The Chancellor might then appoint one of the individuals on the slate. But he might also reject the slate and call for new nominations.

The 1974 Act also significantly restructured university authorities. The membership of the Executive Council increased from 16 to 21, and the Act specified more explicitly those categories of individuals who were eligible to serve (see Figure 2, Chapter 2, for a flow chart of recruitment and voting pathways). For the first time teachers on the postgraduate campus and two colleges principals, hereafter Marathas most frequently, who were elected by the Senate attained representation on the Council.

The composition of the Senate changed and increased in size. Positions that were *ex officio* in 1948, such as principals from rural colleges and heads of university departments, among others, were now elected from among themselves. The number of lay individuals who represented business, labour, registered graduates and various levels of government increased. For the first time, students gained representation, and the number of teachers increased from 5 to 25.

The faculties now included representatives from the Senate, Academic Council, and the chairman and four members from each Board of Studies. It continued to elect the deans of the various university faculties.

The Academic Council acquired additional members from the teachers, especially from the colleges, and college principals.

The Act significantly reorganized the Boards of Studies. This was a loss to the postgraduate campus. Campus personnel could no longer be assured that they would chair a Board of Studies as the 1948 Act prescribed. The 1974 Act required the chair of a Board of Studies to be elected from the membership of the Board, all of which were now dominated by personnel from the rural colleges. The composition of the Boards made their membership an important resource to garner for elections. Since most members were Marathas, the potential for control of university government shifted from Brahmans to Marathas.

Various university and non-university constituencies, such as college principals and postgraduate students were required to elect representatives to university authorities from among their membership. But non-university constituencies also had to register with the university in order to nominate legally their members for seats on the authorities. Some university politicians, such as the Professor, made sure that they had a voice in who these constituencies nominated. In this way the Professor, in particular, gained considerable support from the non-university constituencies.

In general, the Vice-Chancellor lost some power. The Executive Council became the most powerful body in the university. This made it even more essential for the Vice-Chancellor to establish a coalition within the Executive

Council to be an effective administrator. The interests of the postgraduate campus were represented better because two postgraduate teachers and a postgraduate department head gained seats on the Executive Council, and other postgraduate campus personnel could be elected to it in other ways. For example, among the deans who were elected by the faculties, one also was elected by the other deans to serve on the Executive Council. At one point when he was elected dean prior to the 1978 elections, the Campus Leader was elected to the Executive Council from among the deans. The Senate lost some power. It no longer elected the Vice-Chancellor from a slate of names recommended by the Executive Council. It became more of an advisory body to the Executive Council. Still, it placed several persons on the faculties, and two principals and seven other persons from among its membership on the Executive Council. The Academic Council put three persons on the Executive Council.

The Boards of Studies remained the fundamental conduit to offices in university government. As noted, because elections to various boards and authorities followed sequentially and did not require a person to relinquish one office when elected to another, an individual who was elected to a Board of Studies could be elected to various offices, including the Executive Council, in short order. In effect, the Act established the potential for an interlocking directorate. The recruitment of so many rural college personnel to authorities meant that whoever had their support had considerable leverage in the structure of university government and could control the Executive Council and the government of the university at large. This is how the Professor acquired his power and influence.

New Agents in the Arena: The Clique and The

Professor

Despite the fiasco related to the Vice-Chancellor of 1970-1972, the 1960s and 1970s were good years for the Gang. The CC Leader retained considerable support from his Brahman allies in the rural and city colleges. His power and the influence of the Gang seemed unassailable. Its members travelled frequently, had a wide network of potential support, and collected significant travel and daily allowances for these and other activities, such as reading examinations. The Gang had close contact with members of the state legislature. It controlled significant committees, such as that which disseminated examinations to be read. Still, the CC Leader did not develop his largesse and patronage as well as he might have. Nor did he work much at expanding his support base. Emerging political agents were not so lax.

A new university government was elected to office in 1975. The CC Leader and the Professor were returned to the Senate and they and three members of the Clique were put on the Executive Council. The period between these elections and the elections scheduled in 1978 was one of contention, strategic manoeuvering, and girding up for the elections of 1978. Still, while other leaders were actively building their teams and support bases, the CC Leader rested on his laurels and existing support. The university's contradictions were about to erupt.

The Clique

The Clique grew out of routine social relations that developed on the postgraduate campus during the 1950s and early 1960s. Postgraduate teachers were fewer then and more collegial. They were not yet motivated to political action against city college domination of university government. But, as the city colleges basked in the security of their hegemony and control of university government, discontent was growing among postgraduate teachers. It does not appear that anyone in the city colleges was aware of this, or cared much.

Gradually, a dozen or so individuals – they referred to themselves as a Asocial group" – began to organize in the late 1960s. This was the origin of the Clique. Its major goal was the destruction of the Gang. When the Clique emerged as a nominal entity in the 1970s its composition was fixed and would not change appreciably for the next several years, until it came time to divide the spoils of their victory. Although many people on the postgraduate campus referred to the Clique as "the Marathas", it was not overly Maratha in composition. And even within the hard core bloc that comprised the Clique, not everyone agreed on its composition. Some people on the campus were identified as members of the Clique even though they denied it strongly. This ambiguity persists.

Nonetheless, of those individuals who comprised the core of the Clique around 1970, two were CKP, two were Maratha, and seven or so were Brahman. Of the latter, all but one, the Campus Leader, a Chitpavan, were "outsiders" who came either from other states or from the northern districts of Maharashtra. This cadre of agents forged alliances with other outsider Brahman teachers and Maratha principals from rural colleges who now were eligible to sit on the Executive Council.

By the early 1970s the growth of the university resulted in an increased number of teachers on the postgraduate campus. Most teachers came from outside Maharashtra. The Clique wooed them as allies against the city colleges and many supported it strongly. It was a natural alliance. Outsider Brahmans learnt quickly that they needed protection from abuses by Pune Brahmans in the city colleges (see Appendix, Episodes Three and One) and the Clique needed allies. But there were conditions attached to this alliance.

The Clique permitted outsiders to hold offices and positions of influence. But those who held them were suspect, even among some older members of the Clique, by virtue of being outsiders. They were clearly subordinate to the Marathas, CKPs and Brahmans that constituted the original Clique. They were allowed to play a significant role in university politics as long as they abided by the expectations of the Cliques leadership. If they did not, they were replaced quickly, relegated to political insignificance and overlooked for perks, such as promotions. None could aspire to the office of Vice-Chancellor.

Regardless, they received considerable benefit from the alliance, such as protection against abuse. And they expected to share in the spoils when the Clique took control of university government. Most believed that it would. The spoils included promotions, appointments, travel, largesse and patronage. Some opponents of the Clique added graft.

The Campus Leader worked sporadically during the early 1970s to gain support for the Clique among Brahmans and Marathas in rural colleges. But his source of recruitment was narrow. He focused primarily on physics departments. Some of his practices were laudable, such as the seminars he convened to enable postgraduate teachers to inform rural teachers of the latest ideas in physics. But some of his activities also were self-serving. He packaged taped programs in physics and sold them to college departments at considerable profit to himself. Nonetheless, because of his efforts and those of some other members, the Clique did establish a relationship with rural Maratha colleges that was closer than that which the rural colleges ever had with the city colleges. Rural college personnel, for example, often compared the hospitality they extended to personnel from the city college on their occasional visits to rural colleges to the rather shabby treatment they received when they visited city colleges.

The Campus Leader and Clique eventually curtailed these outreach efforts. There were two reasons. The Campus Leader withdrew gradually from his work among the rural colleges to focus his attention on organizing the Clique on the postgraduate campus. And during the late 1960s and early 1970s the Professor was actively building wide support among rural Maratha teachers and managements. Recall that around 1976 the Campus Leader and Professor agreed to divide their spheres of influence and interest. The Clique gave the Professor *carte blanche* to develop support among the rural colleges. The Professor assured the Campus Leader that he would not interfere with the Clique's efforts to organize support on the postgraduate campus. They agreed to work together to defeat the Gang. The test of this alliance came with the selection of the Vice-Chancellor in 1978. The CC Leader wanted to be the next Vice-Chancellor. So did the Campus Leader.

As the Clique consolidated its influence on the postgraduate campus, the Campus Leader worked to make his goal of becoming Vice-Chancellor credible to supporters. The Clique believed that the election of the Campus Leader as Vice-Chancellor was the necessary first step in abolishing any vestige of city college control over the postgraduate campus. Towards this goal, and within proscriptions imposed by city college agents in government, the Clique recruited new faculty to the campus, established departments and programs and sought funds from the UGC to develop student hostels and housing for the faculty. Its leaders studied the 1974 Act thoroughly and learnt how to manipulate its stipulations to their advantage for the next elections. They also kept their alliance with the Professor in repair. They knew that they would need his support in the rural colleges if they were to displace the Gang from university government.

The Professor

Organizing support in the rural colleges was only one activity that engaged the Professor in the early 1970s. He also spent considerable time and resources defending himself and his college in Lonavala from the Gang, the Teachers' Union, and the friend of the CC Leader in state government who coveted the college. The Professor's fight with the union continued for over two years. The litigation with the CC Leader dragged on for over a decade. The schism this created between the Professor and his antagonists was deep and enduring.

After losing his seat on the Executive Council in 1970 the Professor set out in earnest to build support in the rural colleges. He rationalized his project as a moral commitment to improve the education of students and the working conditions of rural college teachers. (Like the CC Leader, morality was an important value in his project.) As he put it, "There is little concern in the university for the problems of the rural colleges, and someone has to look out for their interests." He gradually colluded with the Clique in governing the university and through his considerable support in the rural colleges he became overwhelmingly influential in its government. One city college principal summed up succinctly the Professor's influence when he asserted in a speech in 1982, "There is no VC, there is no EC, there's only NC" (There is no Vice-Chancellor, there is no Executive Council, there's only the first two initials of the Professor's name.) The comment resonated with the Professor's friends and foes alike. It was quoted widely.

The Professor's support extended beyond the rural

colleges. It cut across caste divisions and incorporated a wide field of university categories: college managements, principals, teachers, students, registered graduates, university department heads, administrators and clerks. The registered graduates of the university provided his first base of support in the late 1950s. As his influence in the university increased, so did their benefits. Some received contracts for university concessions and contracts for work. Their children got special attention while enrolling for university programs, and perhaps having their grades adjusted.

College principals represent management's interests in the university, such as keeping teachers in line and ensuring support for management's political candidates. They can make working conditions better or worse. By 1986 about 80 per cent of rural college principals supported the Professor (see Appendix, Episode Three for an exception). Much of this was due to the control the Professor had over appointment's to committees, and he usually complied with managements choices. Such appointments are important links in the flow of the Professor's patronage and largesse. Principals were heavily represented on the examination committee which the Professor controlled. They were able to approve or disapprove a teacher's appointment to committees or influ-ence their appointment or election to university authorities from which he or she might garner travel and daily allowances.

The Professor's largesse and patronage also extended to the postgraduate campus and members of the Clique, from which, of course, he acquired additional support. The Professor worked hard to insure the appointment of his allies as department heads. They also comprised an important voting bloc from which he might gain (see Appendix, Episode Two).

In one case, for example, he engineered the promotion of

a woman teacher in the Hindi Department, who supported him. With his help she skipped the status of reader and moved directly from lecturer to professor, and then to head of her department over other qualified individuals. Shortly after that he saw to it that she was elected to the Executive Council. She lost that seat subsequently because her department refused to confirm her as professor after her probation, a move about which the Professor could do nothing.

Nonetheless, the case is instructive. It demonstrates on the one hand the power the Professor derived from his support. On the other, it shows that he does not win all his battles (also see Appendix, Episode Two), only most of them, at least until 1989.

The Professor had four to six teachers in each college who were staunchly loyal, and in the most northern district of the university's jurisdiction where his power was strongest he had even more (recall that around this time the university had a total of 173 colleges of which 125 were rural colleges). They constituted a voting bloc of between 600 and 900 individuals. No one else in the university had such a concentration of support. Each university authority required teacher representation. And their votes translated into support for the Professor's project. For example, recall how important Boards of Studies, which are dominated by rural colleges, are for election to higher office. As noted, by 1985 the Professor's people controlled 48 of the university's 52 Boards of Studies.

He developed a special relationship with coaches of college sports. They supported him because he improved their salaries, a goal the union never attained. And no one questioned their considerable travel, daily maintenance and equipment expenses. Since they travelled with their teams, they also provided the Professor with a network of communication throughout the university. Coaches and their teams, especially wrestlers, also provided a certain amount of muscle should the situation require it. This was a resource that rural politicians utilized on occasion (Rosenthal 1977). The Professor never required their help. But in 1986 when there was considerable tension on the postgraduate campus over a hotly contested election that involved one of the Professor's candidates, athletes appeared and stood around in clusters. They claimed that they were on campus to campaign for the Professor. Finally, since many of the university's past graduates supported sports teams, the Professor's support of the team enhanced his status with that constituency.

The Professor was conscientious about maintaining his support and keeping his network in repair. He travelled frequently among the colleges. He went out of his way to befriend junior teachers. He tried to meet each new teacher personally. Senior teachers were more likely to be skeptical of his efforts.

He also rewarded his followers well. The largesse he extended came from the same sources that were used by the CC Leader: travel and daily allowances while serving on authorities and committees and examination duties. But the Professor developed and extended it more widely. One teacher in the mid 1970s earned 2,490 rupees in one year, the equivalent of an additional three months' salary, for attending 19 meetings. He claimed that he could have earned as much as 4,000 rupees.

Examinations *per se* may not be quite so lucrative. But if, in addition, the teacher also receives travel and daily allowances to come to the postgraduate campus or some college to read them, the amount earned can be significant. The Professor insured the circulation of these rewards among the teachers who supported him.

An indeterminate number of students were loyal to him, for he provided them with critical services. Eleven committees in the university dealt with student-related matters – admissions, programs, examinations, grievances and the like. The Professor's people controlled most of them. For a fee, some reportedly as high as 5,000 rupees, he insured admission to programs that were closed, higher marks on failed examinations, degrees that otherwise would not be granted. Student athletes benefited from the travel and daily allowances they received as they moved to sports venues. Administrative staff also were involved in the flow of largesse, for they required a reward to accommodate the Professors wishes, such as changing a student's grade.

As noted, the Professor is quick to point out no one other than himself, including the union, looked out for the well-being of teachers in the rural colleges. But in addition to lavishing attention on teachers, he also took advantage of the growth of the colleges to focus on the needs of some categories that managements and the union ignored, such as coaches and librarians. His manipulation of rural college teachers, staff, students and management to provide him the resources by which to pursue his project are a testament to his political and leadership skills.

In 1985, through his control of the Boards of Studies and the support of people he helped get elected to the faculties, the Professor was elected dean of the science faculty, his wife as dean of the education faculty, and others of his supporters to other deanships. With their support he was elected to the Executive Council. Through his alliance with the Clique it appeared that anything was possible. For example, on one occasion a member of the Clique, a professor, wanted to be head of his department. With the help of the Professor and Clique he was elected to the Board of Studies upon which the existing head of his department had a seat by virtue of his position as head. During the subsequent election the aspiring head was elected to the faculties and then as dean of the faculty of his discipline. From that position he made the life of the existing head of his department so miserable that he resigned. At that point the aspiring head resigned as dean and the Clique insured his appointment as head of his department.

As a result of his support the Professor, and ultimately the Clique, gained effective control of university government. This happened primarily, as the CC Leader acknowledged, because they learnt the implications and potentials of the 1974 Act better than he had. The stage was being set for the next phase of the university's dialectic: the resolution of the institutional and, in part, the caste contradiction the city colleges represented in the university.

See Appendix, Episode Three: This episode overlaps the era of the Gang and the era of the Clique. It began in 1973 and, for all practical purposes was not resolved until the protagonist of this episode retired in 2000 (here it covers the period 1973-1980). It is a classic example of how the local Brahmans tried to sustain the dominance of their prestigious city colleges over the postgraduate campus and preclude outsider Brahmans from acquiring positions of authority in the university.

VI

Chapter

The Gang vs the Clique: The Era of the Clique

Introduction

The 1974 Act was the first major threat to the political dominance of city college Brahmans over Poona University. City college agents had long and vigorously upheld the Brahman intellectual traditions for which Pune and its colleges were justifiably famous. They extolled the venerable traditions of the city colleges. They emphasized their relationship with notable Brahman social reformers and political thinkers and activists, such as Ghokale, Tilak, Sarvarkar and others. They promulgated the excellence of the education the colleges purveyed in the service of a greater India.

They also co-opted the primary symbol of Maratha greatness, Shivaji, in an attempt to promote a sense of Brahman-Maratha unity. Personnel in the rural colleges and on the postgraduate campus thought of this as a politically motivated ploy that Pune Brahmans had used in other contexts to appease Maratha resentment (Omvedt 1976; O'Hanlon 1985). Few non-Brahmans among my informants took seriously the attempt by city college Brahmans to establish Shivaji as a univocal political and caste symbol. They were aware that Pune Brahmans and city colleges staff thought of him – and, vicariously, Marathas in general – as an upstart

Sudra peasant. Busts of Shivaji and dramatic pictures of him on horseback are commonplace in rural areas, including the colleges. They are far less evident in Pune. There monuments to Brahman heroes prevail.

While rural college managements have not been especially responsive to teachers' needs, today Marathas in general perceive education to be significant in promoting Maratha political economic development. The attitude that Marathas bring to education is pragmatic, intentional, and more politically than pedagogically directed and motivated. While Marathas resent Brahman cultural and political hegemony, they also know that displacement of Brahmans in the university is not likely – despite their contribution to the 1974 Act. But they also know that their political control of the university may be possible, although this has yet to be realized fully. While Marathas dominate critical university authorities and represent a formidable agency, the highest ranking agents in the university government remain Brahman. Marathas depend on them for leadership and provide through their votes and support a power resource for Brahman leaders, especially the Professor. There has been talk for sometime of one Maratha or another from the rural colleges challenging the power of the Professor. It is an extremely difficult accomplishment, and no one attempted it until 1989. And he was not a Maratha.

Teachers and staff on the postgraduate campus gradually became aware of the preeminent status the campus attained in the university. Many also grudgingly acknowledge that this status is due largely to the political agency of the Clique. Not all faculty members agree with the Clique and its activities. There is discontent with the negative image the postgraduate campus has acquired in Pune because of the Clique's actions and alleged corruption. Yet, the Clique has been responsible for the creation of the postgraduate campus as a symbol for an enclave of elite scholars who purvey a quality education that distinguishes the campus from both the city and rural colleges. In effect, the postgraduate campus has provided the structure through which the political agency of the Clique redefined the place and significance of the campus in the university.

The current alignments in the university are the result of historically constituted practices that for all practical purposes began around 1970. The 1974 Act was the mechanism that unleashed those practices. The Act provided the means for agents on the postgraduate campus to break the hold of the city colleges over the university and establish an alternative vision of the university that was more in compliance with that of Dr Jayakar's than of city college Brahmans. If the 1974 Act was the means that enabled this process, the selection of the Vice-Chancellor in 1978 and the fight between the Gang and Clique in 1982 for ultimate control of university government were the final events in this dialectical drama. These events also culminated in adjustments in power relations after the Clique acquired control of university government.

The Clique: Perceptions

Around 1970 the "social group" that crystallized as the Clique began to revitalize the ideology that embodied Jayakar's vision of the postgraduate campus. This alerted postgraduate teachers to their potential and place in the university. The increasing success of the Clique in wresting control of government from the city colleges engendered a harmony among campus teachers that had not existed previously. Hostility toward the Clique on the postgraduate campus developed slowly from teachers who, as we shall see, suffered either because of their opposition to the Clique or in the division of the spoils once the Clique took control of university government.

The negative image the postgraduate campus today exists because the Clique's activities offend many teachers who are not active in the university's politics. Still to others, such as outsider Brahmans and non-Brahmans, the Clique represents a defence against the potential tyranny of others on the campus to whom they are subordinate, such as Pune Brahmans or department heads. For most, the potential of this tyranny is preferable to falling again under the control of the city colleges.

Most postgraduate teachers are not well informed about the Clique and quite detached from university politics, despite opinions on it that they provide freely. They are involved in their lives and work and identify themselves proudly as members of the postgraduate campus, or university as they think of it. Even some alleged supporters of the Clique are not fully aware of the Clique's organization, motivations and actions. Yet, in some instances they have allocated considerable blame to the Clique through spurious associations that mystify university power relations. Attempts to sort out these realities is reflected in the constant discussion of university politics by those who are actively involved, knowingly affected and perhaps, consciously aspiring to participate.

The political agents involved in the conflict become visible in the faction fighting that ensues around critical periods, such as elections to university government. People on the campus discuss and dissect these fights and the agents involved over and again. They compare and contrast the actions of the university's political agents in terms of the good they provide the campus and that which they provide the agents. The contradictions in caste and institution are not always obvious and people often deny their existence, especially those related to caste. This is done less among those teachers who have a deeper historical understanding of caste relations in Maharashtra. Nonetheless, the general perception of the teaching, research and other work that takes place on the campus *cum* university by its staffs and teachers is positive. The dialectical conflicts that engage the university's politicians are, for the average non-political individual, a slight annoyance at best.

1974-1978

Immediately after the state legislature approved the 1974 Act, steps were taken to replace the Vice-Chancellor and Executive Council appointed by the Chancellor in 1972 and install a new university government in accord with the provisions of the Act. The first Vice-Chancellor appointed under the Act's provisions was a Pune Brahman and Principal of Fergusson College. Elections for offices in university government followed immediately. In those elections four members of the Clique won seats on the Executive Council. These included the Aspirant, the CC Leader and another person who was a Saraswat Brahman. The fourth was a Maratha who would become Vice-Chancellor in 1978. The Professor was also elected to the Council. He was not very influential at this time. But he sided with the Clique to oppose the Gang on most issues.

Despite the Clique's gains on the Executive Council, the Gang retained a majority. There were few changes in university policy at this time. Neither the Gang nor the Clique nor the Professor understood the full implications of the 1974 Act's provisions for controlling university government. But the Clique and Professor were learning quickly, and with their people in place they had a good base from which to build. Throughout this period, members of the Clique met constantly to discuss problems and devise strategies to defeat the Gang. The Professor provided the most original interpretation of the Act: "If the Act does not exclude it, we can do it."

The Clique initiated a series of innovations and developments on the postgraduate campus around 1976 that built upon and consolidated its achievements over the previous several years. It established leadership training programs in various departments. It obtained funds from the UGC and state government to develop department programs, especially in the physical and natural sciences. It developed the interdisciplinary schools favoured by the Campus Leader. It experimented with a semester system instead of year-long courses. And although final examinations continued to be distributed to outside readers, mid-term examinations now were graded by the teachers who were responsible for teaching the classes. The Clique established a "Distance Education Program" to reach out to villages to promote rural development.

The leaders of the Clique placed their close supporters, "talented individuals" as they referred to them, in critical support positions, such as heads of departments and on crucial university committees, like those related to recruitment of new faculty. To obtain additional support they dispensed rewards selectively. These included access to better housing, resolutions of problems and funds for travel in India and overseas. They were important steps in the entrenchment of the Clique in university government and administration. These practices resulted in at least one supporter of the Clique in almost every department on campus. In some departments all the teachers supported the Clique. Thus providing a formidable power base.

These gains were not achieved without cost and duress.

The Clique faced resistance from the Brahman lobby, that diffuse, vaporous category of individuals in Pune, the city colleges and on the postgraduate campus that coalesced at various times to try to thwart the Clique (see Appendix, Episode Six). The Brahman lobby on the postgraduate campus did not necessarily support the city colleges. They simply resented the Clique's tactics and alleged corruption. They justifiably accused the Campus Leader of favoring and directing resources to the natural and physical sciences at the expense of other disciplines. The Clique recruited and supported outsider Brahmans rather than local scholars. The "talented individuals" that they placed in critical university authorities were widely thought to be poor scholars and "yes-men" to its leadership; "second-raters" was the term most commonly applied to these individuals by the Clique's opponents. As time passed some initially ardent supporters of the Clique turned against it.

The Gang and CC Leader still dominated the Executive Council. When and where they could, they tried to block every move made by the Clique. Nonetheless, the Clique realized many of its goals because of its organization. After 1970, when the Campus Leader emerged as a force to contend with, it worked at developing its infrastructure. Gradually the entrenchment of the Clique's supporters in postgraduate departments began to pay off. Heads of campus departments dominated the Boards of Studies, the initial stepping stone to higher office in university government. Even when the composition of the Boards of Studies began to change in subsequent elections, the membership came largely from the rural colleges and supported the Professor. Under his growing influence they served the Clique's interests and helped put its members on critical university authorities. They also helped the Professor extend his influence over the Clique and university government.

The new Vice-Chancellor, recall he was a product of the 1974 Act, inadvertently aided and abetted the Clique's gains. He was a scholarly and thoughtful gentleman, known and respected for his moral and ethical postures. For example, when he was Principal of Fergusson College he went on a fast "unto death" to protest the errant behavior of the Vice-Chancellor who was elected in 1970. He also proved to be weak, ambivalent and indecisive in decision making. People still tell jokes about him that belittles his vacillations. One, for example, relates that on a clear and sunny day he was walking on campus with an umbrella and scarf around his neck. When asked if he thought it was going to rain or turn cold, he pondered the question for a moment and responded that he would have to consult the Executive Council to find out.

He was especially indecisive when it came to dealing with the aggressiveness of the Clique and its fight with the Gang. He felt that he was caught between forces beyond his control, and he was quite aware of his personal failings in these matters. He realized only after his appointment that he was not adept at political intrigue and was unable to take sides in the fights between the Gang and Clique. This served the interest of those who caught him at times when they required a decision on an issue that they favoured. He usually conceded rather than be drawn into the fight that was sure to erupt in the Executive Council between the Gang and Clique. They were becoming commonplace.

The Gang and Clique were developing strategies and girding up for the inevitable confrontation in the selection of Vice-Chancellor and elections in 1978. The Clique aimed its efforts at breaking the hold of city colleges on the university. The Professor was not yet very active in these strategies. He was busy building support in the rural colleges and quietly putting his people in critical positions of university government. Still, the rural voting bloc he was developing did support the Clique. As a result he also established political credit with the Campus Leader and Clique that he would collect later.

The Gang and Clique were consolidating support where they could. Both teams made many enemies. And neither developed alternatives to their existing leadership. All the potential followers and supporters that each team could draw on had already been co-opted. Since leaders by definition need followers, this seriously truncated any attempts for leaders of other teams or factions to develop, or to replace any of the existing leadership. Alternative factions emerged only during critical political junctures, such as the elections to government offices. But their interests, other than their disdain for the Gang or Clique, were diffuse and their members few and unreliable. They were gnats in the political process, annoying, but sure to fade away with a slight change in political climate.

A new Vice-Chancellor was to be appointed in 1978 and elections to government offices were to be concluded that same year. Instead, for reasons to be discussed below elections were put off until 1979. The CC Leader and Campus Leader each wanted to be the next Vice-Chancellor. Since each was a Brahman, although they represented different Brahman castes, Chitpavan and Deshasta respectively, the fight for this office was rooted less in the university's caste contradiction and more in its institutional contradiction and the immediate issue of who would occupy the office. The appointment of the Vice-Chancellor in 1978 was remarkable for the strategies the Gang and Clique employed to contest for the office. No one foresaw the fateful intervention in this process of political agents outside the university.

At the time the Gang was more politically powerful than the Clique. The support rural Brahmans gave to the CC Leader was secure and the Gang still had its people in place on the Executive Council. The CC Leader had the support of the Education Minister and others in state government. The local Brahman dominated newspapers were sympathetic to him and his college supporters. He had done considerable research on the Clique and knew where its members were vulnerable. Even with the growing support of the Professor and despite their work at building support on the postgraduate campus, the Clique was a clear underdog in the contests for university government that were entered in 1978. The CC Leader drew deeply into his bag of information on the Clique to try to thwart its efforts.

Elections: 1978-1979

It was common knowledge in late 1977 that the Campus Leader's name was going to be one of the three submitted to the Chancellor from which he would select the next Vice-Chancellor of Poona University. In December 1977 police presented the Campus Leader with a charge sheet that accused him of 28 counts of corruption in the university. The charges were filed by the CC Leader. But, for reasons that remain unclear, the police delayed action on the matter. This permitted the nominations for Vice-Chancellor to continue.

In January 1978 the Nominations Committee submitted the names of three candidates to the Chancellor. The slate did not include the name of the CC Leader. He was still trying to manipulate the situation privately. He knew that one of the executive councillors had added the name of his brother, a minor office holder in state government, to the list. Such blatant nepotism is prohibited by the statutes of the Act. Both the Campus Leader and the CC Leader knew that the name jeopardized the entire slate and neither wanted to risk identitifying with it. The Campus Leader attempted to have the illegal name removed by the Executive Council. The CC Leader blocked this attempt and it remained on the list. He then leaked the information of the illegal slate and the charges pending against the Campus Leader to the local press, wrote an article on these matters which the paper published, and informed friends in state government. The Chancellor rejected the slate and called for another.

At this point the CC Leader declared his candidacy and his allies added his name to the new list. This slate, which also included the name of the Campus Leader, was forwarded to the Chancellor. But, because of the charges still pending against the Campus Leader, the Chancellor rejected this slate and called for yet another that excluded him.

Distraught and desperate the Campus Leader conferred with the Clique. Its other leaders, the Aspirant and the Professor, were also tainted with scandals and stood little chance of being selected. They decided to submit the name of the Maratha who had served on the first Executive Council after the implementation of the 1974 Act. He was a young man and a protégé of the Campus Leader. He was unknown, and the university had never had a Maratha Vice-Chancellor. They knew that chances of his appointment were slim. The CC Leader, on the other hand, was well fixed with the Congress Party, and with a slate pending that contained no one with questionable credentials it seemed inevitable that he would be appointed.

The Clique did not sit by passively. It appealed to their friends in state government who advised the Chancellor on their candidate. It also published an article in the local press that denounced the integrity of the CC Leader. They were not optimistic. Then fate intervened.

In 1977 Mrs. Gandhi was defeated in her bid to be installed as Prime Minister. This was the fallout of the Emergency she declared in 1975 and the Congress Party was swept out of office throughout India and replaced by the Bharatiya Janata Party (BJP). The slate of candidates for Vice-Chancellor remained pending as the BJP replaced Congress appointees. These included the Chancellor. In his stead the BJP installed as Chancellor an individual with whom the father-in-law of the Clique's candidate had connections and influence. The new Chancellor appointed the Clique's candidate as the first Maratha Vice-Chancellor of Poona University.

The CC Leader was crestfallen. He said it especially galled him that a "nobody" had been selected as Vice-Chancellor and that every time he addressed him and was required to call him "Sir" the word stuck in his throat.

Because of the delays, elections for university government finally took place in 1979. They were hotly contested by members of the Clique and Gang, especially for seats on the Executive Council. The CC Leader was elected to the Council easily. But, for the first time the Clique acquired a majority on the Executive Council.

However, the Campus Leader lost his bid for a seat. An evanescent coalition of department heads that represented part of the Brahman lobby conspired against the Campus Leader. They were disturbed by the activities of the Clique and the widely known charges of corruption still pending against the Campus Leader. Their candidate, a Pune Brahman, narrowly defeated the Campus Leader. The Campus Leader was nearing mandatory retirement. He knew that he had no possibility of attaining a major university office. In his pique, and with the help of the Clique and Vice-Chancellor, he engaged in a vendetta against those on campus who did not support him. Funds to offending departments were cut, reputations besmirched, jobs lost (see Appendix, Episode Two). Actions such as these defamed the reputation of the Clique even more. At this time the Clique began to change, and not always to the satisfaction of its members.

1979 and Political the Fallout

Following the 1979 elections the Gang remained a formidable force and the next four years were rife with conflict between it and the Clique. Executive Council meetings became shouting matches. Members of neither the Gang nor the Clique enhanced their reputations as scholarly gentlemen. The Clique, in particular, established its reputation for rudeness, abusive behaviour, and brutal tactics to gain its ends. Still, the Clique gradually displaced the Gang and gained control of university government. It did not accomplish this without resistance. But with a Maratha Vice-Chancellor, a majority on the Executive Council, and the help of the Professor the Clique increasingly entrenched its authority. Correlatively, support for the CC Leader waned and the power of the Gang dissipated.

In 1982 the Maratha Vice-Chancellor was reappointed. It was the first time since Jaryakar (1948-1956) that a Vice-Chancellor succeeded himself. This cemented the Clique's control of university government. In the subsequent elections the CC Leader contested for the seat of dean of Science. Recall that in the hierarchy of deans this was the highest position and had some power and influence. He ran against one of the Clique's formidable leaders, the Aspirant. By this time the CC Leader's support in the city and rural colleges had either dissipated under pressure from the Clique or had been co-opted or neutralized by the Professor. With the help of the Clique the Professor had managed to acquire all critical sources of patronage and largesse in the university. Deprived of access to these sources of reward the CC Leader had little to offer to potential supporters. Despite an expenditure of 50,000 rupees of his own money, the CC Leader was defeated soundly. He retired from the university's arenas and political field to manage his college. He continues to deplore the existence of the postgraduate campus.

With their apparatus of support in place the Clique fully infiltrated university government. The Vice-Chancellor has considerable latitude in making administrative appointments. Over the next four years he replaced Brahmans in university administration with non-Brahmans. With a few exceptions, such as the Registrar, these were not especially powerful positions politically. Much of the administration remained in the hands of Pune Brahmans. Nonetheless, those who were antagonistic to the Clique raised the frequently heard alarm that the Marathas had taken over the university.

More important to the control of the university than administrative appointments was the ability of the Clique to dominate appointments to positions of influence, especially committees concerned with recruitment and appointments, and to control sources of patronage and largesse. The Clique's supporters became heads of the university's standing committees concerned with campus housing, stores, the canteens, admissions, examinations and the printing press. Some members of the Clique benefited from these appointments by being promoted rapidly after having been denied promotion when the city colleges were in power. Recall that the Aspirant had been a lecturer for almost 20 years and moved quickly to professor and head of his department. The Clique took control of university offices and programs, such as the college development offices and athletics. Most of these appointments were forms of patronage and provided access to monetary resources which in effect were important sources of largesse. This led to recurrent allegations of corruption, embezzlement, and graft. The CC Leader, continuing to smart as a result of his defeat, levelled an inordinate number of these charges. Although he no longer was in power, his college was a constituent college of the university and he continued to represent what he perceived to be the "moral conscience" of the university.

The patronage by which the Clique controlled these committees and offices was indispensable to its control of the university. The Clique and Professor used their patronage to an even greater extent than had the Gang to acquire support. The Professor controlled the examination committees established by each Board of Studies. He dictated to whom examination duties would be distributed. Of course, they went to those who provided him support, and he was disarmingly clear why this was so.

"Why should I give examinations to people who don't support me!" he responded rhetorically to my inquiry.

A first-hand account of the Professor's allocation process by a member of the Clique is revealing. It upset and angered him. According to him, the Professor assigned the exams to teachers who did not necessarily have expertise in the exam's subject matter. The Professor seemed to think that one's qualifications as a teacher was sufficient to pass judgment on any subject. Examination duties are the single-most lucrative sources of patronage and largesse in the university.

Allocating travel and daily allowances to individuals is not as lucrative as it used to be. But reimbursement for travel to read examinations, serve on committees, boards or authorities, participate in Ph D oral examinations, or evaluate colleges and their program development provided additional and often considerable rewards. Many on the postgraduate campus resented that only individuals associated with the Clique were provided these rewards.

One source of patronage extended to the United States. A close friend of the Clique had obtained a position in a small American University near Pittsburgh, Pennsylvania. He acquired considerable funds in dollars from American government agencies to establish an affiliation and exchange program with Pune University. This program sent several American scholars to Pune University to work with the Clique in developing programs, such as those associated with the Education Media Research Centre (EMRC). But it is another irritant to many on campus because it has served as an exclusive conduit for members of the Clique to visit the United States (see Episode Six for one result of this relationship).

Opinions regarding the Clique vary widely on the postgraduate campus. Some think the Clique is excessively abusive. Others, who resent it, concede that it has done some good, especially in establishing campus autonomy from the city colleges. Most are indifferent.

The Clique's composition is conceptualized differently among campus personnel. The number of people who either support the Clique passively or are not openly hostile to it has remained relatively stable. But its active membership is a fluid and changing organization as power relations among its leaders and close followers fluctuate.

From its inception until 1979 the Clique had a relatively stable membership. It had a common cause against the Gang. Once the Gang was defeated close supporters of the Clique began to claim rewards for their services in this endeavour. Dissension developed when leaders could not or chose not to comply with these expectations. Others were disappointed in the division of the spoils. These events caused the first crack in the Clique's facade.

Different members of the Clique wanted different things. Some expectations were modest. A few wanted nothing more than to be heads of their departments. The Clique generally accommodated them. Others wanted to hold office in university government or administration; almost any position could be used as a stepping stone to higher office. These too were easily provided. Of course, this meant that they then had to comply with the goals of the Clique.

In a case that was nearly as famous as that depicted in Episode two, an outsider who had supported the Clique wanted to be head of his department. Another outsider, a "loner" who was not politically active was head. He had a reputation for "eve teasing". Because of one questionable incident the Clique brought charges of immorality against him. The Aspirant claimed that one young woman was so offended by the actions of the head that she broke down in his office while making the charges. As with the head in Episode Two, the Clique saw to it that he was dismissed from the university and that its supporter became head of the department. The dismissed professor found a position of equal status in another university.

This event caused another member of the Clique, a CKP, to withdraw from it. He claimed that the accusation was unfounded and the punishment too harsh. Curiously, he would have supported another charge by which the head could have been replaced. But he felt that the charge of immorality was too severe; a stain on one's character that was hard to cleanse.

The Clique helped another outsider Brahman get elected as dean. Once in office he tried to work independently of the Clique. Just as he was elected with its help, the Clique insured his defeat in the next election.

What people on campus remember most are the events during the few years following the defeat of the Campus Leader for a seat on the Executive Council. They were marked by what people recall as a vicious retribution against those who did not support him and simple greed on his part to insure himself post retirement positions on campus. The Campus Leader promised one associate, a Saraswat Brahman, that he would be appointed head of the College Development Office. But after his defeat in 1979 the Campus Leader decided that he wanted this office. The Maratha Vice-Chancellor had little choice other than to appoint him.

Another member, a Chitpavan Brahman, expected to become head of the EMRC. It was developing at this time. The Campus Leader decided that he was not qualified. Once again he took this position as his own. The rejected member had to be content with a promotion of professor and head of his department.

Heads of three or four departments complained that the Campus Leader – the Clique might be a better referent because the Campus Leader could not have accomplished these strikes without their help – slashed their operating budgets and delayed approval of new positions and appointments in their departments. The Clique's leaders claim that this was a time of budgetary constraint in the university at large and that all departments suffered funding cutbacks and temporary freezes on department development. They point out that department heads do not talk to each other about their budgets because they attempt to maintain any monetary advantage they might have and are uninformed of the bigger picture.

Another individual, a Pune Brahman, claimed that a house that he occupied on the campus university was illegally remodelled by the Campus Leader and divided in two to accommodate one of his supporters. This occurred when the Clique modified policies to insure that housing was allocated on seniority and not rank. The Campus Leader claimed that the house was scheduled to be remodelled in accord with university plans that were established in the early 1970s and that the complainant just happened to occupy that house.

In general, anyone who challenged the Clique was subject to some abuse. The Campus Leader, Professor and Aspirant developed reputations for viciously rebuking anyone who did not accede to their wishes. Rather than comply with the expectations of the Clique or tolerate their abuse, some individuals refused to serve in university government.

One highly respected local Brahman principal of one of Pune's elite colleges won a narrow victory over a member of the Clique for a seat on the Executive Council. Immediately following the election, the Professor and Aspirant met him in his office and informed him about what they expected him to do. He ordered them to leave and resigned his seat. Another local Brahman principal of a highly regarded college refused in 1979 to contest for a seat in university government because of the Clique's expectation of his support.

The Clique's reputation suffered because of these events. Some of its supporters dropped away, disappointed, bitter even, at the discrepancy between what they expected and what the Clique's leaders chose to allocate. Others withdrew because of their outrage over the Clique's excesses.

After the 1982 elections the Clique gradually relaxed it aggressive tactics. The Professor in particular tried to reconcile differences between the Clique, its dissidents and others who were dissatisfied. It was about this time, some say 1980, that the Professor replaced the Campus Leader as the most influential person in the university. According to some people, before 1980 the Professor was vulnerable and his support tenuous. After 1980 his base of support was so broad and firm that he appeared to be invincible. Increasingly his will prevailed in critical decisions regarding the university. Ultimately this resulted in a course of events that radically altered the leadership of the Clique and changed the nature of Poona University's politics.

See Episode Four: This episode, an early event once the Clique defeated the Gang, is a notorious example of political revenge. It shows how a leader can use his political power to nearly destroy a colleague who voted against him, and how caste alliances – Marathas vs. Brahmans – can be drawn into the conflict. This episode is an example of how leaders of the Clique abused their power to reward some of their followers and hurt their opponents once they took control of university government.

See Appendix, Episode Five: The university's political leaders were always scrambling to acquire resources of power. In this episode the same leader of the Clique who starred in Episode four – the Campus Leader – appropriated for his personal uses resources that were made available by a large grant awarded to the university. It was because of his and the Cliques' machinations that the foreign scholar who was responsible for acquiring and managing the grant was drawn into a cabal by dissidents who hoped to depose the Campus Leader.

VII

Chapter

New Agents and Challenges to the Clique

Introduction

The second term of the Maratha Vice-Chancellor ended in spring 1984. His six years in office were a time of exciting and positive changes in the university, at least from the Clique's point of view. They also were a time of excesses that stained the image of the Clique indelibly. Some members of the Clique acknowledged and regretted these actions. But most of them agreed that the excesses were necessary to move the university forward. Nonetheless, disturbing problems persisted and new ones emerged.

The university faced continuing budget deficits. Opponents of the Clique attributed these to the Clique's prodigal fiscal policies. The CC Leader and Brahman lobby continued to level allegations of corruption against the Clique. Newspapers continued to report corruption and scandals in which members of the Clique were alleged to be involved. None were ever proven in court and the Clique brushed off the accusations as just so much political fallout. But some members of the Clique were becoming concerned over the effects of its entrenched power and authority, especially those of the Professor. This concern would lead to adjustments in the nature of university government.

Background

A couple years before the end of the Maratha Vice-Chancellor's term in office a new Chancellor was appointed. He was openly critical of the Clique and the Brahman lobby hoped that he would neutralize it. This did not happen. Shortly after he assumed office the Central government in Delhi transferred him. But two things of note did occur during his brief term as Chancellor. He appointed the Vice-Chancellor that succeeded the Maratha and an amendment to the 1974 Act was introduced in the legislature. It limited the term an individual could hold an office on any university authority to two years. It got bogged down in committee. But it became an important component of the university's politics when the Clique was rebuked and the careers of some of its leaders were destroyed by an unlikely agent, the new VC.

By the end of the Maratha Vice-Chancellor's second term in office the organization of the Clique had altered significantly. The defeat of the Gang restructured the contradiction between the postgraduate campus and the city colleges in favour of the Clique. But it also denied the Clique an important rationale for its unity and purpose. Although people in the university still perceived the Clique to be a monolithic entity, a team, it was rent increasingly by two factions. They represented a mélange of interests and contradictions in caste, region and institution, although they largely excluded the city colleges and their Brahman constituency.

The first faction included the Aspirant, the Maratha Vice-Chancellor, other Marathas on the postgraduate campus and outsider Brahmans. The second faction included the Professor and Campus Leader, rural Marathas, and Pune Brahmans on the Executive Council who owed the Professor favours and supported him. Several factors accounted for this division, especially the contradictions within and between the factions.

The first faction was dominated by the Aspirant, a CKP. The Aspirant always preferred to work quietly, behind the scenes. It was difficult to identify him with the range of decisions and actions that were so commonly associated with the Campus Leader and Professor. But he was effective in recruiting support for the Clique from outsider Brahmans because of the protection and assistance his association with this faction provided them. The Maratha Vice-Chancellor was somewhat marginal to this faction. During his last year or so in office he worked increasingly to disengage from his image as a protégé of the Campus Leader and develop his own career. This faction excluded Pune Brahmans on campus. Other members of this faction knew that their relationship with Pune Brahmans was a product of the general alliance formed to defeat the Gang. With that now behind them, they knew that the historical and regional divisions between them and Pune Brahmans could be stressful if Pune Brahmans attempted to reassert their traditional dominance in the university. The possibility of this was blatantly manifest in the second faction.

The second faction was dominated and led by Pune Brahmans, the Campus Leader and Professor. Each, recall, came from outside Pune. But each was a Chitpavan Brahman and each had been around long enough to be identified as a Pune Brahman. The participation of rural Marathas in this faction represented the caste and regional contradiction in the university. But it also represented the traditional subordination of Marathas to Brahman authority, in particular the Professor because of his control of patronage and largesse. In addition, Marathas' traditional apprehension of the city colleges and postgraduate campus lingered.

A potential schism in this faction existed between the Campus Leader and the Professor. There was widespread and growing concern that cut across all interests in the university with the increasing power of the Professor. He either decided or influenced almost every policy matter brought to the university government. The Campus Leader clearly was losing power to him, although at the time of the appointment of the new VC, he still maintained a relationship with the Professor. This would change soon enough.

Curiously, although he was not aware of it, the Professor was also beginning to suffer an image problem. Despite the rewards they received for their loyalty, some Marathas were beginning to chafe and resent the control the Professor exerted over them. Paradoxically, some of the Brahmans who supported the Professor were commenting that the Professor was becoming a Maratha by association. This was not meant to be flattering; they began to distrust him. These perceptions of a change in his image and status were influential in later events when some of his allies turned on him.

Of the two factions, the latter, composed of the Professor and Campus Leader, was the most powerful and influential. But, it also was the most fragile. The factions often worked together. But just as often the Aspirant and non-Brahman faction opposed the leadership of the Brahman faction. This was most obvious during elections or appointments. The Aspirant increasingly supported candidates who contested against those supported by the Professor.

Despite the tendency for factions to develop and the growing political influence of the Professor, the Clique still constituted an interlocking directorate that dominated university government. By 1984 there seemed to be a consensus in and outside the university, in the state government, for example, that a change in leadership in the university was necessary.

In spring 1984 the Clique composed a list of candidates it favored from which the next Vice-Chancellor would be appointed. The selection committee submitted the list to the Chancellor and he appointed a candidate who appeared to have impeccable credentials.

The New Vice-Chancellor, or VC

The new VC spent most of his career in a government research laboratory in New Delhi where he acquired a national and international reputation as a physicist and scientist. He was also well fixed with people in government in Delhi. He had, for example, met the Chancellor who appointed him and, as some on campus said, "He had walked the halls of power." People on campus thought this was a positive factor. A Vice-Chancellor is required to represent the university nationally and internationally and this background qualified him eminently. But, as events will show, the VC also learnt how to play a mean game of politics in those halls.

Upon his retirement as joint director of the lab he was awarded with the help of the Clique a distinguished chair in the Department of Physics at Poona University. He held this position for nearly two years prior to his appointment as VC. During those years he developed a reputation on campus as a gentleman and hard-working scholar, who was concerned about the well-being of the university. He also was a Chitpavan Brahman and from the same city in northern Maharashtra as the Campus Leader. There was lingering, but not overly strong concern, among some people on campus who were suspicious of Chitpavan Brahmans and recalled the consequences for the development of the postgraduate campus of earlier Brahman

Vice-Chancellors. But it also was widely thought that the VCs background, credentials, and long stay in Delhi would render his caste insignificant in his work. There was widespread optimism in the university that he would provide an antidote to the hegemony of the Clique. The fact that the Clique and, in particular, the Campus Leader supported his appointment did not seem to register with those infected with this optimism.

The Campus Leader was instrumental in hiring the VC and securing his research chair in the Physics Department. The reason was simple. He and the VC not only were born and raised in the same Chitpavan caste community in the same northern city, from childhood they were exceptionally close friends. (Recall the VC's comment in Episode Three: "The Campus Leader is closer to me than my wife.") The Campus Leader had always been well off financially. He helped the career of the VC, who was not so well fixed, in many ways. Subsequent events suggest that the Campus Leader felt that the VC should now repay the debt by complying with the Clique's projects. He seemed to think of the VC as another protégé and product of his paternalism, as the Maratha Vice-Chancellor had been. The VC had different ideas. The Maratha Vice-Chancellor only gradually expressed his independence from the Campus Leader. The VC revealed an independence of action within the first two years of his appointment that discomforted the Clique. He would become a formidable agent with his own project.

After his appointment, the VC had a honeymoon with his Executive Council for the few months during which elections took place to fill university authorities. Following the elections and over the course of his first year in office the Clique made him fully aware of the extent to which it controlled university government and could and would limit his actions and decisions. The Clique expected him to comply with and support their policies, as the Maratha Vice-Chancellor largely had. In turn, it would let him take credit for accomplishments in the university and enhance his reputation. Otherwise it could make him look the fool.

The VC was responsible for his increasing difficulties with the Clique. Like many other university scholars, the VC had not paid close attention to their actions. He thought he could work with it. He soon discovered that the Clique permitted him independence of action only when it did not interfere with its interests. The VC was allowed far less authority in matters related to appointments, promotions, and allocation of resources that comprised the Clique's patronage and largesse.

The Professor was his biggest problem. He had a solid majority in the Executive Council and other critical university authorities. Very simply, he was more powerful than the VC. To compound his problems, the VC allowed his friend, the Campus Leader, to continue as Director of the EMRC and control its considerable resources. The Campus Leader also used the VCs name when it suited him to demonstrate his influence in university government. In part this was because he was losing power to the Professor. It did not take long for an issue to arise and reveal the extent of the differences the VC had with the Clique.

About a year after the VC was appointed, the honeymoon with the Clique ended abruptly in what the Clique thought was an act of rebellion: The VC offered the position of Pro-Vice-Chancellor to the Law College Principal, who was totally unacceptable to the Clique (see Appendix, Episode Three, for details of this event). There were two significant consequences of this incident. One was the offer of the VC to resign over the issue. Under pressure from a broad-based support network that cut across caste, institutional and regional contradictions he changed his mind. Some, however, said his offer was mere histrionics and that he had no intention of resigning.

The other involved the mobilization by the Clique, probably the Campus Leader, of the Akhil Bharatiya Vidyarthis Parishad, or ABVP, and Patit Pawan. These are student wings of the RSS, sometime the RSS (Rashtriya Swayam Sevak Sangh), which is a conservative Brahman-based Hindu fundamentalist organization that appeared in Episode three. A major goal of the RSS is to control India's educational institutions (Anderson and Damle 1987) and it saw this incident as an opportunity to make inroads into the postgraduate campus where its representation was weak.

The VC, perhaps also the Campus leader, recruited the student wings of the RSS to help dissuade the Law College Principal from accepting the appointment of Pro-VC. Students who comprised these wings were happy to comply. The ideologies of the student wings and that of the Pro-VC were diametrically opposed, and the students resented his liberal politics. On more than one occasion the Principal had opposed and reprimanded right wing students in his college. The introduction of the RSS into university affairs inserted a new agency into its politics and augured future events.

This episode revealed the extent to which the VC vacillated between his own goals and subordination to the interests of the Clique; he supported the mobilization of the RSS student organizations even though he knew the Principal was at odds with them. His vacillations became more erratic as he realized the extent to which he would have to humble himself to the Clique's projects.

Following the appointment of the Pro-VC, the VC became increasingly stubborn, inaccessible, unpredictable and unwilling to listen to department heads, university faculty and his own staff. Increasingly he permitted his administrative staff to take care of issues that might be controversial or in conflict with the Clique's interests. He ignored or evaded other issues. Under less politically charged circumstances this may not have been terribly important. But the Professor built his power by paying attention to precisely those matters that other university administrators overlooked or did not control well. He filled whatever vacuum the inattentiveness of the VC created. With little interest in or influence over the array of day-to-day activities in the university, the VC often was required by default to comply with the Clique's expectations, even when he did not agree with them. Sometimes he avoided Executive Council meetings when a vote was required on some important issue that the Clique supported, such as an appointment. This suggested that he disagreed with it. In other instances he seemed to be in bed with the Clique and supported its every decision.

Increasingly his administrative decisions seem designed to infuriate someone and his responses to problems confused his image. Many department heads became upset at his dissembling. They did not know what to believe or expect from him. Funds, appointments, new staff positions, etc. would be approved one day and withdrawn shortly thereafter. Many issues and requests submitted to him withered from his inattentiveness. One directive infuriated almost everyone. He decreed that each faculty member must be in his or her office between 11:00 a.m. and 6:00 p.m., the normal working hours of the university. Faculty complained that he was trying to run the university like the research lab from where he had come.

Many of his actions suggested academic prejudices. He allocated funds that favoured the natural and physical sciences at the expense of the humanities and social sciences. He delegated authority to the Pro-VC to cast votes during his increasing absences from Executive Council meetings.

Some of his actions appeared to be political. He replaced the head of a department who was a Maratha and a member of the Clique with a Pune Brahman. The Maratha was vulnerable. He had just lost a close election for the head's representative on the Executive Council to the Maverick, a Pune Brahman (although he denied caste affiliation) who was not a member of the Clique. The VC claimed that the Maratha had been a head for several years and that he was only exercising the democratic provisions of the 1974 Act that permitted the VC to rotate department heads every three years. Had the Clique supported him, he would have made other changes. The university finance officer, a Maratha appointed by the Maratha Vice-Chancellor, took a leave of absence to avoid working with the VC.

In other cases he appeared to be an active member of the Clique. For many years the university had been affiliated with a consortium of American midwest colleges. By an established agreement the consortium sent American students to the campus for a semester-long learning experience under the guidance of teachers on the campus who it selected (see Haithcox and Smith, 1982, for a description of the program). The Clique claimed that the Americans dictated policy to the university and it wanted more control over the program. The main reason for this was the proviso in the agreement that provided postgraduate teachers who participated in the program the opportunity to teach for a semester or two in one of the American colleges represented by the consortium. The Professor wanted to send one of his supporters to America. The Americans refused because he was not involved in the program and did not speak English. As a result of this debate the Americans transferred the program to another institute. The VC supported the Clique's demands on this issue, in part because he concurred with them. On the other hand, he had little choice to do otherwise. He also acquired a reputation for being anti-American over this issue.

He began to establish relations with the network of influential Pune Brahmans, many of whom were connected to the city colleges, sentimentally in some instances, functionally in others as members of their managements, and politically because of their support of the RSS and the ABVP and Patit Pawan. He was blamed for permitting a research institute with which he had connections to build on university land. Many recalled how the city colleges tried to chip away at the estate the postgraduate campus occupied. But, because title to the estate remained with the state government, Rajiv Gandhi, then Prime Minister of India, instructed the Chief Minister of Maharashtra to give the land to the institute. Many teachers either were not aware of this or chose to ignore it. The transfer of land was blamed on the VC and interpreted widely as an abuse of his trust and a gift to his Brahman friends in the institute.

By the end of his first term in office it also was generally agreed, even by members of the Clique, that he had become involved in some questionable financial matters with the Campus Leader. Rumours persisted that he deposited university funds in a private account for short periods and used the interest for personal purposes.

In general, his haphazard responses to university matters and problems and his vacillating relationship with the Clique confused his image. But there were reasons for his actions. He maintained ostensibly friendly relations with the Clique. In part this was because he often had little choice to do otherwise. In part it was because some issues were not worth fighting over.

But just as often, his reluctance to act was perceived by the Clique as a form of resistance, if not open rebellion. Whether he acted or not, his image was tarnished among people who were hostile to the Clique and who originally thought that he would rescue the university from its clutches. Instead there was a growing sentiment that he was a Pune Brahman who did not have the best interests of the university at heart.

If his actions during his first term as VC seemed erratic and confusing to many, they also added to his mystique. Some attributed his behaviour to hubris, others to an inability to administer properly. Some claimed he was shrewd. One member of the Executive Council insisted that from the perspective of his political acumen he was the best Vice-Chancellor in India. Many continued to think that he was in the hip pocket of the Clique. Still, others thought that he was leading a vendetta against it. Some of his behaviour in the fall of 1986 presaged things to come after his reappointment as Vice-Chancellor in spring 1987.

In fall 1986 his relations with the Clique were so strained that he offered to resign as VC for the second time. The Brahman lobby on Campus and Pune Brahmans in the city colleges strongly urged him to reconsider. Members of Patit Pawan party went on a fast to convince him to remain in office. When he decided not to resign he offered the Patit Pawan students lemon juice to break their fast. This was interpreted widely as a symbol of his sympathy for the RSS. Although Patit Pawan opposed him when he helped to appoint the law college Principal Pro-VC, their support at this time became important later.

In spring 1987 the VC was reappointed Vice-Chancellor. In the elections that followed the power and influence of the Clique increased. Almost all of its people were reelected, and it had a Pro-VC appointed with whom it could work to replace the VC's choice. But there were increasing indications of rift within the Clique.

In the elections for the head's representative on the Executive Council, the Professor increased his control when his candidate defeated one supported by the Aspirant. The Aspirant took the defeat graciously and retired to the background again to observe the unfolding political process. It was a strategy he had pursued consistently over his 13 years in university government. But the increase in the Professor's power upset the VC. Curiously, it was a previous action of the VC that appeared spiteful at the time that permitted the Professor to augment his support.

At this time the Maverick was Head of the Zoology Department and representative on the Executive Council of the department heads on the postgraduate campus. As he had on previous occasions with other department heads, the VC decided to replace the Maverick. This made the Maverick ineligible to serve on the Executive Council. A new election was called. This permitted the Professor to orchestrate the election of his supporter and acquire an additional ally on the Council. The VC's relationship with the Maverick would have significant consequences for university government, and it is worthwhile to consider the Maverick for a moment.

The Maverick complied with the implications of this appellation. He spent 18 years teaching and conducting research in Zoology in the United States and Europe. As a result, he acquired a number of cultural traits that upset many people on campus, including the VC. He was a Chitpavan

Brahman by caste, but denied vociferously any caste affiliation and disdained the entire ideology of caste. He was aggressive, outspoken and unpredictable. He also travelled to Europe frequently, wore jeans and married one of his students. These idiosyncrasies were tolerated because he was a productive research scholar and obtained considerable grant money from national and international research agencies.

The Campus Leader was instrumental in hiring him in 1969 because of his research abilities and because he thought he would be a good ally. Instead, they soon parted ways. The Maverick became an outspoken critic of the Campus Leader because he thought he was corrupt and that his actions hurt the university. He became an active member of cabals to depose him. For example, he participated in a cabal to depose the Campus Leader for misuse of research funds (see Appendix, Episode Five). People on campus assumed that he was antagonistic to the Clique, and when he was elected as heads' representative on the Executive Council some people hoped that he would develop a coalition to depose it. At this time he was identified with the Brahman Lobby.

However, the Maverick was extremely defensive of his department, especially the considerable grant funds he brought to it and the equipment they provided. Even though the Professor was Dean of the Science Faculty in which Zoology was nested, his basic complaint was with the Campus Leader, not the Professor. Largely, this was because the Campus Leader had been instrumental in helping the Clique misuse some grant funds that he acquired for his research and to develop the Zoology department. His project as the heads' representative on the Executive Council was to protect his interests and those of his department. Other matters were secondary.

After he assumed office on the Executive Council people noticed quickly that he did not attempt to develop a coalition against the Clique. He often voted with the Professor. This was because he had established a *quid pro quo* with the Professor. The Maverick agreed not to object to the Professor's activities in university government. In return the Professor agreed not to interfere with the Maverick's departmental affairs, including the grant funds he obtained. Because of this, many people began to identify the Maverick as a member of the Clique. But the Professor knew that he was not a reliable ally. As he told me, "(The Maverick) has no interest in the university. He's only interested in his department and grant money." Still, the Professor did not dislike the Maverick. The VC, on the other hand, detested him. This was because the Maverick was vocal in his accusations of the VC's corruption as a result of his association with the Campus Leader.

Although the VC continued to appear friendly with the Clique, he also wanted to be in charge of the university during his second term. The Clique certainly inhibited this. But his major concern was the Professor. The Campus Leader and Aspirant shared this concern. The Campus Leader was beginning to smart at his loss of power to the Professor, and he began to reassess their relationship.

Around the time of his reappointment as Vice-Chancellor the VC began to introduce new agents into the political arena. They were allies with whom he intended to build his own team to oppose the Clique. One, an ambitious Chitpavan Brahman, was a principal of a city college who many thought was a staunch ally of the Professor. He was the person the Professor nominated and the Executive Council approved as the teacher to go to America under the agreement with the Midwest College Consortium. As noted, the consortium disapproved and he did not go.

The principal aspired to a position on the postgraduate campus. But not just any position. When, as a result of the Professor's influence, he was offered an appointment in a postgraduate department he rejected it. Instead he chose to become principal of a city college whose management was tied closely to the RSS. This was largely because he was an official in the RSS and had close ties with the ABVP and Patit Pawan. Events suggest that he was more committed to the RSS and its goals than to the Professor, and that his secret agenda was to become Pro-Vice-Chancellor of Poona University.

The VC also recruited another ally, a Pune Brahman who also was director of one Branch of the EMRC. It was no secret in the EMRC that the Branch Director coveted the Campus Leader's position as director. Events suggest that he had the ear of the VC and that his strategic position in the EMRC facilitated a process that began a few months after the VC was reappointed.

In July 1987, the VC met secretly with the RSS Principal and the Campus Leader. They concocted a strategy to neutralize the Professor's power. It soon became obvious that the VC had decided that the RSS was a reasonable alternative to the Clique.

The VC was a strong supporter of the Congress Party. It opposed the RSS ideologically and practically. Once his relationship with the RSS became obvious it surprised and disturbed many people. Regardless, once he made the decision to remove the Professor and dispense with the Clique at large events moved rapidly. Over the next five months the structure of power relations in the university were altered drastically. Here's what happened.

A couple of years before all this began the Campus Leader gave some broken equipment from the EMRC to the Professor. He intended to have students at his vocational school in the city repair it to help train them in job skills. The transaction was legal and the proper paper work was completed and placed in the EMRC files. The students, however, never completed the task and the equipment remained at the school.

About a week after the secret meeting with the VC, the Campus Leader announced publicly that the Professor had stolen the equipment from the EMRC. The paper work that enabled the transaction disappeared and the Professor had no way to refute the charge. Although the Professor had always before been able to counter accusations of wrongdoing, this time he was caught with the goods red-handed. Nonetheless, he had a pretty good idea of what was happening and responded immediately. But as he and his son were loading the equipment into a van to return it to the EMRC police appeared and arrested him. This event introduced the RSS into the university's politics.

Patit Pawan students were instructed by the Campus Leader to watch the Professor, and they alerted the police at the proper time. The Professor was their first victim, and their treatment of him was not pretty. Students from the ABVP attacked him in front of the courthouse in Bombay where he went to plead his case before the regional High Court and post bail. While police watched the students blackened his face and paraded him around the area on a donkey, each a symbol of shame and disgrace, while chanting denouncements of his alleged crimes and corruption. Signs that accused him of corruption appeared throughout Pune, scrawled even on the pavement of streets and highways. Patit Pawan students threatened him with bodily harm if he entered the university.

Regardless, the Professor continued to defy them. He would roar on to the campus on his motorcycle to attend Executive Council meetings.

Shortly after that incident RSS students began to harass other individuals on campus with whom the VC had problems. In August, shortly after the attack on the Professor, the RSS abused the Pro-Vice Chancellor that the Clique had installed. The Campus Leader invited him to his flat off campus, presumably to discuss these events. When he arrived, RSS students met him; the Campus Leader was not there. They proceeded to shame and embarrass him by calling him names, insulting him, tousling his hair, and so forth. The incident upset him so badly that he resigned as Pro-Vice Chancellor. Within a month the VC had a considerably humbled and somewhat frightened Executive Council nominate the RSS city college principal as Pro-Vice Chancellor and the Chancellor confirmed his appointment. He had found the niche on the postgraduate campus to which he aspired. It was a good point of departure for the RSS to begin to entrench in the university. Events denied the opportunity.

Following the appointment of the RSS Principal as Pro-VC and through fall 1987 the ABVP and Patit Pawan bullied individuals on the campus with whom the VC had problems. Members of Patit Pawan, for example, threatened the Maverick in his office. He drove them off physically. Many people on campus applauded him for his pluck. Others were more easily intimidated. Executive Council members who supported the Professor were abused publicly. Among others, his wife, Dean of the Education Faculty, was threatened. The Professor's support on the Executive Council began to waver. Some resigned. Whenever an Executive Council meeting was held and the Professor attended RSS students, sometimes more than 200, agitated in front of the Administration Building. The VC finally was forced to call police onto the campus to maintain order. They established a constant presence.

The excesses of the RSS students against the Professor and on the postgraduate campus upset the Campus Leader. He did not expect events to turn as they did. He merely wanted to remove the Professor from his positions of power and help his old friend, the VC. Through him the Campus Leader hoped to insure his influence in university government and his position as director of the EMRC. Events were to turn even further.

It is not clear how knowledge of the equipment transfer that incriminated the Professor surfaced, who came up with the idea to use it against him, and how the paperwork disappeared. But, as noted, it was no secret in the EMRC that the branch director wanted to be director of the entire operation. In late fall of 1987, the VC read a list of charges to the Executive Council that accused his old friend, the Campus Leader, of complicity in the alleged theft of the equipment and of misappropriating university funds. Since the Executive Council still contained the Professor and some of his supporters, albeit a somewhat shaken bunch, there was no sympathy for the Campus Leader. He immediately resigned as director of the EMRC and retired from the university, a very bitter person.

Shortly after the VC made the charges against the Campus Leader public, the ABVP roughed up the branch director in front of the Administration Building. Some suggested that the Campus Leader instigated this. Regardless, he did not become director of the EMRC and eventually took a position at another university. The VC seemed to be reluctant to put anyone into any position of influence that was even remotely related to the Clique. He was not yet finished disposing of it.

The intrusion of the RSS on the campus upset many people in the university and elsewhere, such as the Congress Party which was dominated by Marathas, many of whom had interests in the rural colleges. They certainly were not sympathetic to Brahman Hindu fundamentalists having more influence in the university. For the next several months the VC attempted to reconcile with the university community. He pointed to the discrediting of the Clique as a major accomplishment of his office. Because of his tactics, many people remained suspicious of his motives. Some who disliked the Professor and Campus Leader even expressed sympathy for them. They pointed out that some of their policies had been good for the campus, certainly preferable to those of the RSS. But even while trying to be conciliatory, the VC was still disdainful of those whom he disliked. This was to be his undoing.

During the period of the RSS student agitations the Maverick was negotiating with Hindustan Lever, a major Indian corporation, for a very large amount of money to fund a research project in the Zoology Department. During the course of the agitations Hindustan Lever became increasingly reluctant to get involved with the university. For reasons that appeared to be spiteful, the VC, with the help of the Aspirant whose dislike of the Maverick was mutual, worked to undercut the credibility of the Maverick and to discourage the corporation from funding the project. The Maverick informed the Chancellor of his unhappiness with the VCs actions and Hindustan Lever's concern. In late summer 1988 Hindustan Lever announced that it was withdrawing from the project. Many people, including the state government, were displeased. The VC blamed the Maverick for the situation. But in a display of feigned guilt he offered to resign over the matter.

The VC worked this strategy twice before when he was in difficulty with the Clique. Each time the Brahman Lobby and others in the university and in Pune pressured the Chancellor to reject his resignation. This time the state government was upset and under pressure from a variety of sources to resolve the problems in the university. Hindustan Lever was a strong supporter of the Congress Party, and the government did not want to appear to be cozy with the RSS. In addition, rural colleges informed the government through their representatives in the legislative assembly, primarily Maratha congressmen, that they were displeased with the involvement of the RSS in university affairs. As Marathas, they were ideologically opposed to the Brahman dominated Hindu fundamentalism that the RSS espoused. Even though Pune Brahmans continued to support the VC and pleaded with the Chancellor to reject his resignation, he accepted it, much to the VC's consternation. But the VC also saw the satisfactory culmination of his efforts to dispose of the Clique, at least momentarily.

The VC had lobbied for some time to have the state government enact the statute that prohibited anyone from holding a seat on a university authority for longer that two terms or six years. The incidents on the campus made headlines, and state politicians were disturbed sufficiently to approve the statute in 1988. And they made it retroactive. This required a wholesale resignation from university authorities. On the Executive Council, that included the Professor, Aspirant and all supporters of the Clique. At that point charges against the Professor and Campus Leader were dropped.

After accepting the VC's resignation, the Chancellor appointed, in early 1989, the previous Maratha Vice-Chancellor (1978-1984) to serve as Vice-Chancellor until the next elections in spring 1989.[1] At that time the selection committee recommended the Aspirant as Vice-Chancellor. The Chancellor concurred.

Several factors accounted for the appointment of the Aspirant as Vice-Chancellor in April 1989. He had worked hard over the years to sanitize his reputation for belligerence and vindictiveness. Many people acknowledged his skill as an administrator and parliamentarian. He was knowledgeable of university government. No one else was available with his qualifications and abilities. The university was in such turmoil that few others were willing to take the responsibility of the office. After the chaos of the previous months the state government wanted someone to restore order. The Maratha dominated Congress Party which was incumbent in state government supported him in this charge.

The Aspirant used his skills to restore peace to the university. He was helped because there were no factions to contend with: the Executive Council that was elected after his appointment was devoid of the Professor and his followers. But he had made so many enemies that he remained indelibly stained and his antagonists did not allow him much of a honeymoon after his appointment.

See Appendix, Episode Six: The power and authority of the major leaders of the Clique appeared to be unassailable. They were used to governing the university through vice-chancellors and executive committees of their own making. When one of their hand-picked puppets, a new Vice Chancellor, rebelled and chose his own path they were caught off guard and, ultimately, destroyed by his brilliant yet ruthless and decisive political actions. But in the course of these events, the Vice-Chancellor, like the CC Leader earlier, was himself hoist on his own petard.

Note

1. After the expiration of his appointment as Vice-Chancellor at Poona

University he became Vice-Chancellor in another Maharashtra University on an interim basis. He took leave of that position to accept the interim position in Poona University.

VIII
Chapter
The End of an Era

Introduction

Many people on the postgraduate campus thought the VC had eliminated the Clique by his assault on it in 1988. When I visited the university in summer 1989, shortly after the Aspirant became Vice-Chancellor, the Clique was in an disarray and except for the Aspirant and a few very circumspect supporters, they were deposed from the university government. But during my visit to the university in 1994-1995 it was obvious that the Clique was alive and well, albeit smaller. By 1991 the Aspirant (hereafter I will refer to him as the VCA – "A" for Aspirant) had reconstituted it with himself as the leader of a team composed primarily of outsider Brahmans and Marathas.

During the VCA's two terms in office (1989-1995), the politics that affected the university emanated as it had never before from agencies that were external to the university. These included party politics and policies that involved the BJP, RSS, conservative student associations that were introduced by the VC, and the Congress Party. These agencies remained formidable through the first year or so of the VCA's incumbency and were a nuisance throughout the remainder of his term in office.

Until the second term of the VC who resigned in 1988, the politics internal to the university were restricted largely to the actions of the Clique, its own internal problems, and its fights with the Gang and that nebulous formation known as the Brahman lobby. During the VC's tenure the Brahman lobby became more active in the university's politics and far less nebulous. After 1989 the politics internal to the university emanated largely from the conflict between the VCA and his detractors, most of whom constituted the Brahman Lobby.

The individuals on the postgraduate campus who comprised the Brahman lobby were vocal and identifiable. They included many of the university's best scholars, such as the Maverick. Recall in Chapter 7 the VCA had supported the VC against the Maverick during his negotiations with Hindustan Lever. Additionally, the Lobby included a cadre of teachers who were the campus's traditional dissidents. They felt that in one way or another they had suffered from the Clique's policies. Other members of the Lobby came from the city colleges and the Brahman community in Pune. Some of them were elected and otherwise served on various university boards, authorities, commissions, and review panels during the VCA's terms in office. These agents relentlessly colluded and conspired during the VCA's incumbency to try to force him to resign. The Lobby claimed that he was corrupt, not a scholar, and, even more vocally, that because of him "Marathas had taken over the university." Since the Clique produced no obvious heir to the VCA the Brahman Lobby believed that if he were removed from office the Clique would dissolve.

However, the Brahman Lobby could not force this agenda because it was disorganized and leaderless. Its members on campus did not get along with each other or those in Pune. The campus's top scholars did not especially like each other and all of them thought that most of the campus dissidents who were members of the lobby were "second raters," and "obsolete" as one referred to them. Alliances with Brahmans in the city were improbable because they threatened to involve Brahmans from the city colleges in campus affairs and no one wanted that. These schisms inhibited the lobby's effectiveness and denied it any chance of deposing the VCA. But it provided a persistent and nagging opposition that he and the Clique could not ignore.

Still, many teachers who were not politically involved supported the Clique's responses to the lobby's unrelenting attacks. One highly rated scholar, a CKP, stated unequivocally, "Brahmans are manipulative and devious, and if they are having problems today, they're of their own making. Historically they have survived well by their cunning, and the dislike of them is well deserved." Another, a Muslim, complained that the A(VCA) is only one man and the problems he faces are the same all over India. He represents Poona University, and when the Brahmans attack him, they attack all of us in the university. Those who were antagonistic to the VCA and the Clique believed their cause to be just and were just as adamant that their agenda to force the VCA out of office was good for the university.

External Politics

The politics external to the university was grounded in two separate agencies. The first resulted from a law enacted by the central government in Delhi that required the reservation of positions in Indian universities for scheduled castes and scheduled tribes (hereafter simply scheduled castes).[1] The second agency emanated from politics as practiced by Maharashtra's Congress and Bharatiya Janata Parties and attempts by party agents to influence university government.

Reservations

In the late 1980s the Central government in Delhi established a commission to review the reservation of occupational and other positions in Indian society for scheduled castes. The Mandal Commission, named after the member of the Lok Sabha who was appointed as its head, recommended major revisions in reservation policy and extended reservations to categories that previously were excluded. Mandal, as the commission and its recommendations were known, became law in 1992. As a result, Indian universities were required to reserve 50 per cent of their open positions for teachers and students to individuals in those categories that were identified on the revised schedule.[2] By 1994 appointments to faculty teaching positions in the university were a contentious issue.

According to Mandal, scheduled caste individuals who were eligible to hold faculty positions in the university were identified on a roster, or list. If the roster did not contain the name of a qualified scheduled caste individual who the university could try to recruit for the open position, the university was required to advertise the position to attract a qualified person. Individuals who were not on the schedule could be awarded the position permanently, subject to confirmation after two years, only after it had been advertised five times.

Individuals who held ad hoc positions on the postgraduate campus, mostly Brahmans, were bitter. Many contended that the Clique was hostile to them because they were Brahmans, maintained that recruitment procedures were unfair, and that they were manipulated by the Clique. They complained that if they were not in favour with the Clique, it had ways to insure that they would not be appointed permanently.

Theoretically the administration could do this in two ways. It could extend the number of times an ad hoc appointment was made, thereby extending the time during which the search for a qualified scheduled caste individual could continue. The administration could also manipulate the position's reserved status. It was nearly impossible to alter the names on the roster. But Brahmans alleged that the committee that managed the roster was controlled by the Clique and that it changed open positions to reserved positions if it did not favour a candidate. Evidence for use of this latter manipulation was thin, and interpreting Mandal to check the feasibility of these alleged irregularities was difficult. But the Brahman Lobby claimed that qualified individuals, read Brahman candidates, were being exploited and deprived of permanent positions.

Supporters of the Clique, the Registrar and others administrators argued that those who complained of unfair hiring practices either did not understand how the roster worked or simply were out to discredit the VCA. They pointed out that it took time to find qualified scheduled caste individuals. Even some detractors of the Clique stated that the VCA was scrupulous in complying with Mandal. However, some Mandal appointees on the postgraduate campus had Master's Degrees only. The Brahman Lobby argued that they were not qualified to be postgraduate teachers.

Almost everyone agreed that compliance with Mandal lowered the quality of university education because scheduled castes lacked educational skills. It was true that Scheduled Caste students throughout India had a difficult time adjusting to the demands of a university education.[3] But the quality of educationprovided by Scheduled Caste teachers was more difficult to assess. Poona University's Brahman Lobby claimed, with little solid evidence, that scheduled caste teachers provided an inferior education. But supporters of Mandal asserted that even if this was so, which they denied, the recruitment of qualified scheduled caste personnel was justified and necessary to rectify ancient social inequalities in India. Those who disagreed with Mandal pointed out that affirmative action laws regarding reservation policy and equal employment opportunities had been around since the early 1930s and never worked.

The presumed decline of the quality of education at the university had another dimension. The commentary on the inferior quality of scheduled caste teachers was not asserted publicly. It was a sensitive issue, fraught with some pity (as well as contempt) for the scheduled castes and spoken about delicately. Much more up front and vocal was the frequent assertion by the Brahman Lobby that "Marathas have taken over the university." This was because the VCAs Clique was largely composed of Marathas, and thecontempt many Brahman teachers had for them was thinly veiled. The Brahman Lobby in particular drew invidious comparisons between what it perceived to be the VCA and Maratha's lack of scholarly credentials. The Lobby placed considerable blame on the VCA for what it argued was the decline of education standards and quality in the university. It complained in the media that he did not provide the model of the scholar it believed should occupy the post, and as the appointment of the new Vice-Chancellor approached in 1995, editorials in local newspapers pleaded for a "scholar" to occupy the office.

Party politics

Poona University was never totally free of political party influence. Recall that most rural colleges were established by Maratha politicians who used them as political resources. After Marathas assumed control of the Congress Party in Maharashtra the managements of city colleges, largely Brahman, increasingly affiliated with and supported conservative parties, such as the BJP. But until 1988, with the exception of the appointment of the Maratha Vice-Chancellor in 1978, neither party overly influenced university government. The invasion of the postgraduate campus by student organizations associated with the BJP and RSS in 1988 was a watershed for political party involvement in the university. This event was a reflection of larger, national party politics.

From the mid-1980s the BJP seriously challenged the national hegemony of the Congress Party. Because Pune was a Brahman stronghold, its Brahman community provided the BJP with considerable support.[4] By 1987 the managements of Pune's most elite colleges were affiliated with the BJP. Recall that the city college Principal with RSS credentials became the VC's Pro-Vice Chancellor and student agitations began around this time. The agitations on the campus by students who were affiliated to political parties in 1987 were annoying. But they were not very important politically.[5] Two issues caused this to change in 1988: the revocation of the university's authorities by the state government and the lowering of the voting age to 18.

The party politics that had implications for the organization of university government was initiated when the state government made the revocation of the university=s authorities in 1988 retroactive to include those who were elected in 1987. Recall that this action forced everyone out of office who held a position in university government for two years or more. At that time the Clique appeared to be effectively deposed.

In the elections to reconstitute university government in 1988 individuals with partisan party affiliations acquired representation on the Executive Council, Boards of Studies and other university authorities. The reconstituted Executive Council was comprised almost exclusively of individuals serving for the first time. It included one member of the Clique and seven representatives from rural college managements and principals who still had ties to the Professor. These individuals were identifiedas the "insiders." The Chancellor appointed several individuals from both the Congress party and BJP. He hoped to balance party affiliations and check any sentiments the insiders held for the Clique. Other individuals who had party affiliations, largely with the BJP, came on as representatives of outside constituencies, such as the past graduate association. As a result, the Congress Party and BJP representatives became inordinately influential in university politics.

During that next year-and-a-half or so Executive Council meetings were a hot bed for partisan wrangling.[6] Representatives of the different constituencies, in particular the political parties, had agendas regarding policies, appointments, finances, affiliations with colleges, and the like that threatened to alter the social structure, organization and culture of the university. Individuals with *RSS* sentiments, for example, were particularly interested in gaining control of the library and its resources. That would provide a major means of information control regarding their agenda. Other interests wanted to restore the prominence of the city colleges over the postgraduate campus. Some conspired against the appointment of the Aspirant as Vice-Chancellor. A few conservative Brahmans spent considerable time denouncing the VCA and trying to thwart his every policy and action. These diverse interests provoked fighting in the Executive Council and the conduct of university business suffered badly.

All of this was exacerbated by increased student agitations. Until 1988 political parties supported student candidates who might become future party stalwarts. When the voting age was lowered to 18 political parties took a new interest in student politics and government; student cadres now could be recruited for immediate service to party interests. As the VCA saw it, "Poona University became a vote bank of 185,000 students" for which the parties competed. Political parties began to support individual students for offices in student government in the hope of obtaining their votes and loyalty to party interests. Even though all students were free to run for offices in student government, those with partysupport were most likely to be elected.

In 1988 student agitations became extreme and threatening. It was not uncommon for hundreds of students to converge on the postgraduate campus during Executive Council meetings to protest those with whom they disagreed and support those who represented their party. The selection of the Aspirant as VC provided a cause célèbre for conservative student protests. In the first year of his incumbency students trashed his office and openly ridiculed and threatened him. Threats were enough plentiful and ominous for the state government to provide him a body guard.

Student demonstrations became so serious that in 1990 the University Senate amended those statutes of the University Act that codified the procedures for student elections. The amendment permitted only the very top students of each class to compete for offices in student government. This largely eliminated the influence of "hooligan" elements in student government that were allied with the political parties. In their last hurrah over a thousand students confronted the VCA when he visited a rural college and demanded that he rescind the amendment. He refused and under police protection, left the college. There were no more agitations.

By the end of the VCA's first year in office in spring 1990 university government had returned to a semblance of normality. In addition to the decline of student demonstrations, dissident executive councillors gradually resigned, were not re-elected, or were otherwise deposed. But through the VCA's two terms in office, conservative party interests in the Brahman Lobby were more persistent in university government than anytime prior to 1987.

Internal Politics

If there is truth to the adage that politicians are justifiably paranoid because some alternative political team is always waiting in the wings of the political stage to show that it can do the job better than the incumbents, then the VCA had reason to be paranoid. The Brahman lobby's attempts to depose him were relentless. This goal set the tenor of the politics internal to the university for the six years of the VCA's incumbency.

The university's second political agency emanated from the Clique's politics. The consequences of its politics from the perspective of the campus denizens who paid attention to university politics can be summed up succinctly. By the end of the Aspirant's tenure as Vice-Chancellor, the Clique and its supporters thought that conditions in the university had never been better. The Brahman lobby and others of the Clique's detractors thought that conditions in the university had never been worse. The truth lay somewhere in between.

Despite the Brahman lobby's allegations, the confrontations between it and the Clique lacked the internecine potential that marked the conflict between the Gang and the

Clique, and the Clique and the VC. Much of the effort expended by the Brahman Lobby to dispose of the VCA can be likened to sniping. It was a constant annoyance, but hardly fatal to the Clique's work, much of which was beneficial to the university. The Brahman Lobby persisted in near total denial that anything good transpired during the VCA's tenure. Facts prove otherwise.

During his two terms in office the VCA enabled a variety of positive changes in the university. Perhaps most significantly, by the end of his second term, and for the first time in decades, the university budget showed a financial surplus. This was an important accomplishment because by the early 1990s neither Maharashtra nor the central government via the UGC had the resources to support higher education as they had in the past. The VCA found other ways to improve on and build the university's net worth. These included frugal management, soliciting grants-in-aid and endowments, shrewd investments and restructuring university bank accounts.

"Privatization," as it was referred to, also spread throughout Indian higher education. In Poona University, as elsewhere, larger departments and professional programs, such as economics, business, medicine, engineering and the like, were required to pay their own operating expenses, including salaries, in some instances. Poona University, like others, increased student fees to cover expenses. Income from foreign student fees was especially lucrative. Even the VCA's detractors could not deny that by the end of his incumbency the university was financially independent.

By 1994 the most common complaint against the Clique was summed up tersely by one of its opponents: AThe Clique is made up of too few people with too many portfolios.@ Some members of the Clique agreed. For example, one prominent member of the Clique, a Maratha, was Head of his department, head of college development, a powerful position for distributing largesse in the form of travel and daily allowances, head of an interdisciplinary school, dean of the Social Sciences, a member of the Executive Council, and official spokesperson for the university. He admitted that his duties were a burden and stressful.

Another Maratha, the Pro-Vice-Chancellor, was widely unpopular, even with some members of the Clique. Prior to his appointment he had been a long-time executive councilor and principal of a rural college. He spoke English poorly, was crude in his manners, had a reputation for being anti-Brahman and allowed his wife to sell produce from their farm to wives on campus, which his sons or he himself delivered, often with his bodyguards in tow. Some members of the Brahman Lobby complained that this was unprofessional behaviour. Some of their wives, on the other hand, appreciated the service. Nonetheless, this practice sorely offended the sensibilities of some campus Brahmans. But even more distressing was his tendency to act rashly in ways that re-enforced his image as anti-Brahman and the Clique's hit man.

One of his more nefarious actions received considerable attention in the local press in 1993. When the VCA was away he ordered the finance officer to withhold the pay cheques of two Brahman department heads for failing to comply with an order from the registrar.[8] Upon his return the VCA conceded that a mistake was made and they were reimbursed. But the Pro-Vice-Chancellor's reputation for guile was enhanced.

The centralization and narrowing of university government authority under the Clique was largely a defensive response to the increasing attacks by the Brahman Lobby against the VCA. A major consequence of this centralization of government was a reduction in sources of redress available to teachers. The original Clique included several individuals to whom people on the campus with problem is could go for help or advice. At that time the Clique's diversity provided university personnel with checks and balances and allowed them to manipulate the system somewhat to their advantage. The VCA's Clique was so busy and often suspicious of other's motives that university personnel found it nearly impossible to meet its members. By 1995, with no sure source of redress for their problems, people felt alienated, demoralized and apathetic which they had not previously. The conflict between the VCA and the Brahman Lobby increased the teachers' malaise.

The frequent reports in the local press of the university's every problem did not help the morale of teachers. One editorial emphasized how the university's political problems tarnished its image as the "Oxford of the East". Regardless of how the university's reputation suffered as a result of reports in the local media, most people in the university supported the appointment of the Aspirant as Vice-Chancellor. They were happy to have a VC who was able to restore order on the postgraduate campus and re-establish normal university business.

For the first year or so of the VCA's incumbency the Brahman Lobby had no major issues with which to attack him. During this period lobbyists on the Executive Council had to be content to heckle him, belittle his policies, and iterate what became their mantra: "The Vice-Chancellor is not a scholar!" Issues emerged soon enough which provided the Lobby ammunition for its project to force him out of office. These issues can, be divided into three categories: those that involved his responses to problems in the university, those that smacked of the Clique's retribution and vengeance, and those aimed at enhancing and retaining the authority of the VCA and Clique vicariously after their incumbency ended.

The Marks and Plagiarism Scandals

In December 1990, about a year and half into the VCA's incumbency, the son of his family physician failed his final exam in a medical college. Prior to this he was an exemplary student, and many thought that the assignment of the low marks – only 17 out of 100 – was deliberate. The VCA complied with the student's request, one of 15, to have his exam re-evaluated. But, unlike the other 14 students, the VCA expedited the re-evaluation of his exam and had it hand carried to the University of Bombay for re-evaluation. On this reading and a subsequent re-evaluation the student received a respectable pass.

The Brahman Lobby cried fraud and favouritism and argued that the failing marks should stand. It appointed committees to evaluate the situation and pleaded its case to the Chancellor and courts. The Lobby appealed the student's revised grade for over two years. The student's passing grade was upheld on all appeals.

Ultimately documents surfaced that suggested the incident was a conspiracy by two influential Chitpavan Brahmans with long and deep grudges against the VCA. While the "marks scandal" dragged on, they and the Lobby found other issues to pursue, such as the case of plagiarism by two teachers on the postgraduate campus. The Lobby claimed that this incident demonstrated the VCA's lack of scholarship and leadership.

In December 1992 the Editor-in-Chief of The World

Journal of Microbiology and Biotechnology informed two Poona University teachers and their Ph.D. student that reviewers rejected the paper they had submitted for publication because it was plagiarized. In April 1993 the teachers apologized to the editor and to the VCA with whom they met after he was informed of the issue. They blamed the student and said they would debar her from receiving her Ph.D. The VCA wrote a letter to the editor and apologized for the fraud on behalf of the university. He apparently thought the issue was over. It was just beginning.

Shortly thereafter the teachers were forced into other admissions. One, that they and the student had published another plagiarized paper in *The Indian Journal of Microbiology* in 1990; second, that a reviewer had questioned the validity of the student's Ph.D. dissertation in May 1991 and, finally, that in May 1993, he rejected her dissertation because he discovered that some of it was plagiarized. On February 5, 1994 the Editor-in-Chief exposed the plagiarism publicly in an editorial in *The World Journal*. The VCA's response to this disclosure was deficient.

He wrote to the Editor and told him that he had just been informed of the plagiarism and was shocked to learn of it. This obviously was not so. Realizing the gaffe, the VCA tried to rectify it. Instead he made other contradictory statements. He claimed at one point that he had forgotten about the matter. On another he said that he thought the issue was subjudice and therefore inappropriate to comment on.

Regardless, on February 23, 1994 the VCA admitted to the Executive Council that he had been informed of the first plagiarism in 1992 and about the second, earlier plagiarism only later. He argued that he simply forgot that he had written the first letter to the Editor-in-Chief and that the second admission by the teachers had confused him. The Council accepted his explanation and appointed a three man committee to investigate the matter.

When the VCA's ins of omission and commission became public the Brahman Lobby, led by the two Brahmans who were in the forefront of the marks scandal, had new ammunition for their goal to force him out of office. Most teachers on campus accepted his explanation and thought he was guilty at best of being short-sighted and tardy in his response. As a result of the findings of the investigating committee, in September 1994 one teacher was fired. The other, an older man, was retired. The student immigrated to the United States and was not awarded the Ph.D.

Vengeance: The Teachers' Forum and the Female Professor of Hindi

The Teachers' Forum is an association of teachers on the postgraduate campus. It has a Board of Directors and an Editorial Board that publishes *The View Point,* a newsletter in which teachers may comment on university issues. In 1993 the Forum's Boards of Directors and editors were co-opted by discontented teachers that comprised the campus component of the Brahman Lobby.

Prior to 1993 university politicians ignored criticisms in *The View Point.* For example, both the Professor and the VC disregarded criticism in *The View Point* of their actions. But in January 1993 the four editors of *The View Point*, each a Brahman professor, one of English, published an especially inflammatory, crudely worded and provocative issue. They itemized alleged corruption, mismanagement, misuse of resources, scandals, abuses of privilege, etc, which they attributed to the VCA, Pro-Vice Chancellor, Registrar and Clique in general. Many teachers agreed with some of what they said. Much of it was business as usual in the university. But everyone was embarrassed by the meretricious and vulgar grammar in which they adduced their argument. People wondered how a Professor of English could allow a comment, such as "The sign of the University of Poona is pig and recently asses," to pass review. He claimed the other editors printed the issue before he read it. His reputation, already questionable, suffered more.

The VCA, in particular, took umbrage at the criticism, and most people thought that his response was disproportionate to the provocation. He threatened the editors with a law suit for defaming and maligning the image of the university. According to the law, charges of insubordination can be brought against an employee who can be proven to slander or otherwise defame another or the institution. The editors were not aware of this prior to publication. After publication they were quickly apprised of it. They defended their comments as their right of free speech.

Most people, including some members of the Clique, thought the VCA should let the matter drop.[9] As one iterated, these individuals were already "obsolete." Many teachers felt that the VCA's response smacked of the vindictiveness with which he was identified previously. One of his very closest and oldest allies commented that he was punishing the editors for the years he was slighted for promotion by city college Brahmans. The fact that he was also involved in litigation against another Brahman teacher, a woman in the Department of Hindi, gave this conjecture some credibility. We met this woman, staunch supporter of the Professor, in Chapter 5.

Recall that around 1986 she was, with the help of the

Professor, promoted to professor and appointed Head of the Department of Hindi over other qualified men. She then quickly, also with the Professor help, won a seat on the Executive Council as the head's representative. In that election she defeated another head who was a close friend of and supported by the Aspirant. However, when, in 1988, her department refused to confirm her position as professor she lost her position as department head and her seat as head's representative on the Executive Council. She soon found herself in legal trouble with members of her department. Her problems were exacerbated after 1988 when the Professor lost power and could not support her. Ultimately members of her department itemized 15 charges against her. These included misconduct, negligence of duty and moral turpitude for acting against the interests of students and the university. They and some members of the Clique insisted additionally that she was rude, pushy, argumentative and incorrigible.

Almost all the women teachers on campus, as well as many men, were upset by the charges. They claimed that she was "being hounded", the victim of a misogynist administration who resented her because she was an aggressive woman. Some felt that the VCA was retaliating because she defeated the candidate he supported for the Executive Council in 1988. One suggested that this was the VCA's last battle with the Professor. The VCA denied this. He pointed out that all the charges were made by members of the Hindi Department and that he was required to act on their behalf.

In February 1995 the Executive Council found her guilty of 11 of the charges and dismissed her from university service.[10] The charges pending against the editors of *The View Point* died when the VCA's incumbency ended a month later.

Boards of Studies: How to Insure an Election

Recall two items: first, that each discipline in the university is represented by a Board of Study which establishes the syllabus and parameters of offerings in that discipline; second, that Boards of Study are important politically; chairmen of Boards of Studies, for example, can be decisive in the election of deans of faculties.

According to the University Act a Board of Study requires 11 teachers from the discipline it represents. However, some smaller disciplines, such as Sanskrit, ancient history, microbiology, anthropology, defense studies and others cannot support that many teachers. The Act provides two alternatives to rectify this situation. In one, teachers may develop a syllabus for the discipline they represent and seek approval for it from the Academic Council. In the other, the Vice-Chancellor can appoint *ad hoc* Boards of Studies for these disciplines. Such Boards must be comprised of not more than five persons, two of whom must be outside representatives of the discipline under question. These boards have tenure for two years.

There is, precedent for each practice. But when the VCA appointed 20 or so *ad Hoc* Boards of Studies the Brahman Lobby made it an issue.[11] Although the issue became public in the local newspapers in March 1993, it arose a year earlier, in March 1992, shortly after the appointment of the VCA to his second term. At that time a member of the science faculty lost an election as dean to a member of the Clique. The loser challenged the election in a letter to the Chancellor. He claimed that the VCA influenced the election when he put 50 of his supporters in place to by creating 10 *ad hoc* boards of Study. In April 1992 and through subsequent exchanges with the Chancellor, the VCA defended his action by pointing to precedents for the practice. He claimed that the Boards were in the interest of the university because disciplines that are under-represented deserve representation. The VCA's detractors claimed that he packed the boards with people who were loyal to him to insure the election of deans he favoured.

Whatever the reason, and the Lobby=s complaint had credibility, the VCA's actions were legal andthe Boards stood, as did the election of one of his close supporters to the Dean of Science Faculty, the highest ranking Dean in the university. Even though the appointment of the next Vice-Chancellor was, at that time, nearly three years away, a newspaper article suggested that his successor should have the right to make the appointments to the *ad hoc* Boards. This was an oblique slap by the Brahman Lobby at his competence – and cunning – for the Clique always knew the intricacies of the Act better than its opponents.

On February 10, 1995, Foundation Day, Poona University celebrated its 46th anniversary. The VCA announced in a speech to a gathering of teachers and staff in front of the old administration building that the name of the university was now, as prescribed by the 1994 University Act, Pune University. Beyond announcing that official name change, the speech was tactfully selective and subjectively insightful.

He made no mention of the Vice-Chancellors who were lauded by Pune's Brahman community for their distinguished service to the university. Instead he referred only to Dr Jayakar, a kindred CKP. He asserted that the university had attained its national and international reputation because of Jayakar's perseverance in laying the foundation upon which his vision of the university as the Oxford of the East could be built.

Notes

1. The constitution of India includes a schedule, or list, of castes and tribes that are economically and socially disadvantaged. They are entitled to specific benefits. Untouchables, or Harijans, or Dalits, as they are commonly called now, constitute the bulk of the Scheduled Castes (Nyop 1985).
2. As a result of the Mandal commission the percentage of reservations for each category was scheduled castes 13 per cent, scheduled tribes 7 per cent, nomadic tribes 11 per cent, and other backward communities 19 per cent.
3. By 1995 frequent newspaper stories identified problems, often tragic, such as suicides, that befell college and university students from scheduled castes. The culture and secondary education available to many of these students did not prepare them for the rigors and challenges of college work.
4. In addition to the Brahman support upon which conservative parties, such as the BJP, relied traditionally, the BJP also was building considerable support among the non-Brahman middle class business community in Pune.
5. As a result of the disturbances the state legislature expedited the 1994 University Act. It restricted the Vice-Chancellor to a single five year term, increased the power of the office, reduced that of the Executive Council and renamed it the Management Council. I have retained the previous name for the sake of continuity. Recall that the 1994 Act was not important to this work.
6. This period included the four to five months (December, 1988 to April, 1989) following the resignation of the VC during which the previous Maratha Vice-Chancellor (1978-1984) served as interim Vice-Chancellor, and the first year or so following the appointment of the Aspirant as Vice-Chancellor in April 1989.
7. Although this was not the direct result of the Clique's policies, two of the university's northern districts were detached and restructured as the new Northern Maharashtra University. This made Pune University smaller, less costly, and easier to manage.
8. The local press argued that the Registrar also was complicit in this order. Teachers on the postgraduate campus blamed the Pro-Vice Chancellor.
9. Around 500 students and 160 teachers appealed in writing to the VCA to drop the charges.
10. She was still in court appealing her dismissal in March 2002.
11. The number of ad hoc Boards the VCA actually appointed is ambiguous. Some say 10; a local paper said "20-odd," others reports said 30 or 36. The VC-Aspirant was not sure how many he appointed.

Epilogue

Chicanery, dirty tricks, character assassinations, hegemonic lies, deceit, abuses of power, personal ambitions, revenge – they are among the stuff of politics wherever it is practised. The politics of the agents involved in the struggles to govern Poona University was no exception. Given the politics that embroiled so many in the university for so long, what can be said of its outcome?

Many thought education would suffer. It did not. Many thought that Marathas would take over the university. They did not. Many thought the political fights of its leaders and intrusion of politics external to the university would destroy it. They did not. Some continue to trumpet the subordination of the postgraduate campus to the city colleges. That will not happen.

Instead – despite whatever one may think of the politics of its leaders – Poona University grew dramatically in intellectual and scholarly stature, pedagogical excellence and research quality when measured by the standards of institutions of higher learning in India. The "research schools" initiated by the Campus Leader are thriving and serving the university well. New programmes and departments enhance the university's pedagogical and research offerings. Qualified teachers, despite allegations to the contrary and in the face of problems presented by Mandal, staff these programmes and departments. Very competent and creative Vice-Chancellors strive to insure that the university's curriculum, teaching, research commitments and service to Pune meet the challenges of the twenty-first century.

In 2001, the UGC proclaimed Pune University a "Centre of Excellence". It is one of four universities in India to attain this status. The men and women who participated in this study and the politics in which they engaged, in all its ramifications, helped to make this so.

Appendix

I

Episode

How to Put an Opportunist in His Place

The episode represents an incident in which concerned individuals turned a relatively innocuous incident related to the Maratha wars of the seventeenth to nineteenth centuries into political capital. The entire episode lasted only a few weeks in 1985-1986. But it was replete with symbolic and ideological testament to the behaviour expected of an outsider Brahman on the postgraduate campus. Although no one ever proved it, many people suggested that the Clique manufactured this incident to humble a dissident.

The individual involved was head of the department of Defence Studies in which he had a chair endowed by the Sarvarkar Society, established to honour V. D. Sarvarkar, an illustrious Pune Brahman and revolutionary during the freedom struggle. The Sarvarkar Society expected the philosophy of their *bahadur* to be the focus of study in the department and wanted the position filled with a local Brahman. When no qualified individual could be found, the Clique appointed the current head, an outsider Brahman, in 1982. Over the years he came to be viewed with some derision on campus. He was flamboyant, loud and a wit who constantly made quips about individuals and events in the university and elsewhere. Many, especially the politicians, considered him to be pretentious, ambitious, egotistical, and an unreliable ally. None of them knew the high esteem in which he held the university, a factor that was important after this episode concluded.

It began when the Executive Council received a letter written in Marathi from the Sarvarkar Society. It complained that the Head was "anti-Maharashtrin" and levelled several charges against him that were more fluff than substance. They asserted that he was hostile to Maratha students; believed the Maratha wars of the seventeenth through nineteenth centuries were so much nonsense; didn't teach classes; didn't speak Marathi and wouldn't learn it; favoured non-Maratha Ph D students; caused Maratha students to drop out of his department; and, finally, that his department was a subsidiary of the American Center in Bombay. The letter demanded clarification of this connection. It urged the Executive Committee not to confirm the Head in his position, even though he had been confirmed for several years. Many people thought the letter was intended more to admonish and reproach than to destroy him.

An incident between the Head and a Ph D student in the department triggered the letter. The student submitted a dissertation written in Marathi that dealt with the Maratha wars. The letter accused the Head of telling him that the history of the Maratha wars was irrelevant and that he should have taken a more contemporary problem and written the dissertation in English. (Students have the option of writing their dissertations either in Marathi or English.)

The student was related to the family of one of Maharashtra's eminent Maratha chief ministers and he had considerable support for the research from different local politicians, Brahmans and non-Brahmans. Both Brahman and

Maratha politicians manipulated the symbol of Shivaji, a Maratha hero who was discussed in Chapter 2, and the Maratha wars, to their political advantage. They encouraged him to research the topic and write the dissertation in Marathi. They told him that there would be more local interest in it and it would benefit local students. They provided him with a grant to conduct the research and support publication of its outcome. Whether the politicians were involved in this episode is moot. It seemed unlikely that the issue was important enough to occupy their time. Besides, the student defended the Head, although not publicly.

He said that in his experience the Head did not oppose Marathas and that he suggested that he write the dissertation in English on a more contemporary topic because it would be more helpful to the students future Career. The student considered that to be sound advice. He claimed that certain people misunderstood the Head's remark, and that he may have got into trouble due to his demeanour.

After the Executive Council received the letter the Vice-Chancellor reviewed it and it was discussed in the Senate and Executive Council. For a few weeks, while these reviews were going on, the Head was in a dither and discussed the letter's implications extensively with his colleagues and friends. People began to speculate about who was behind the letter and why. The Head had acquired a reputation for cozying up alternately with the Clique and those opposed to it, depending on how his interests might be served. Many thought that the Professor was the instigator because the Head's political machinations and vacillations upset him, and because some rural college teachers were supposed to have complained to the Professor that the Head was arrogant and rude to them. Others blamed the Campus Leader because the Head had been in a cabal to discredit him (see Episode Five). Still others claimed that it was because he boasted about casting a vote that cost a member of the Clique an election. This was the only tangible incident that could be attributed to him.

In the elections following the appointment of the VC in 1985, the seat for the Head's representative on the Executive Council became an issue of special contention. A member of the Clique held the seat. The Maverick and another Pune Brahman who had been a member of the Clique and was now out of favour challenged him. The Pune Brahman entered the race as a spoiler without much hope of winning. At that time the Maverick was extremely outspoken against the Clique. Many people on campus thought that he might be the one to lead a revolt against it. On the first ballot the spoiler received two votes, the incumbent 13 and the Maverick 12. Since the electoral rules require that a clear preference be made between two final candidates another vote was scheduled. The spoiler agreed to give his votes to the Maverick, and on the final ballot the Maverick defeated the incumbent 14 to 13.

Although the ballots were secret, the Head immediately boasted that he supported the spoiler and therefore tipped the balance in favour of the Maverick. However, the loser also claimed that the Head approached him and offered him his vote if he would support him for the position of dean of his faculty, which he refused to do. And after the election the Maverick claimed that the Head approached him for favors because of his support. The Head's boastfulness and manipulations did not endear him to anyone.

After a couple of weeks the VC informed the Head that he was going to dismiss the matter. The Senate and Executive Council did so as well. Still, one consequence of the review of the matter in these governing bodies was a public analysis of the Head's personality and behaviour. Much of it was not becoming. Although he was humbled somewhat after his exoneration, whenever a situation permitted, the Head continued to allude with a feigned bravado to his role in defeating a member of the Clique. And since he was personally convinced that the Professor had written the letter, he became even more critical of him.

During my visit to Pune University, in 1989, I talked to the Aspirant who was then Vice-Chancellor. The topic of the Head came up in some context and the Aspirant made some deprecating comments about him. I pointed out that of all the individuals with whom I had spoken during the course of my research, the Head was the only one who never once made a disparaging remark about the university. He might criticize its politicians – everyone did that. But to the Head, Poona University was sacrosanct. In 1994-1995 when I visited the university the Head's star had risen considerably. He held important appointed positions on committees and governing bodies and people now listened to what he had to say, even though he persisted in injecting his ironic wit and humor into his comments.

II

Episode

Games People Play...

This episode concerns the appointment of the Head of the Department of Mathematics on the postgraduate campus. Among other things, it reveals how deeply embedded symbols related to caste and politics are in the university. Events tend to support the contention that political conflicts in the university are issue oriented. This episode, however, reveals that any specific situation may be influenced by a variety of factors, many of which are historically constituted and embedded in the university. The episode reveals how knowledge of the provisions of the University Act can be brought to bear on an issue, even in an apparently irrational manner. Finally, it reveals how grudges could be forgiven by the Clique as it strove to get on with the business of governing the university.

The appointment of the Head became a contest between individuals who supported two different candidates for the position. One was a rural Maratha who had an appointment as Reader in Mathematics Department at a Maratha University. The other was an outsider Brahman who had an appointment as Reader in the Mathematics Department on the postgraduate campus. Neither had any special relationship with the Clique; either candidate could have been acceptable to it.

The outsider Brahman had been a Reader for many years. He had a reputation of being a good scholar and not politically active. The Maratha's background was more varied.

He taught in three Maharashtran universities and spent six months as a Visiting Professor at a Hungarian university. He also served as Principal of a rural Maratha College. It was in this capacity that he had problems with the Professor and the Clique. He was one of the 20 per cent of rural college Principals who did not support the Professor's politics.

College management appointed him Principal in June, 1982. Just before that he was teaching at one of the state's Maratha Universities. The Executive Council does not usually get involved in college appointments. But the Clique did object to his appointment, although not very strenuously, because of the college's history.

A dynamic Maratha individual started the college. He managed over time to offend a lot of people. He deserted the Congress Party after independence, became active in a Marxist party in the 1950s, and continued to hold strong Marxist sympathies. Neither the Gang nor the Clique sympathized with such a political posture and he had trouble with each. In the late 1960s he blew the whistle on a misappropriation by the management of a rural college that had connections with the Gang. He also did not get along with the Professor.

In 1977 he decided to open a college and made the appropriate application to the university. If a college complies with prescribed standards, and here it did, approval is usually quick and easy. His college received approval five years later, in 1982, after considerable hassle, especially from members of the Congress Party.

He became chairman of the college's managing board and shortly after it opened he had the Maratha, an old friend who he knew as a student, appointed as its Principal. The Professor did not support the appointment. But the Maratha received some help from the Aspirant in this matter. It is not clear why the

Aspirant supported him. But a reasonable hypothesis is that factions within the Clique were beginning to form and this represented one of the challenges by the Aspirant to the Professor's power and influence. They would increase.

In early 1984, a power struggle took place in the college. Another Maratha candidate who was especially close to the Maratha Vice-Chancellor at that time replaced the chairman. The principal's position now was precarious. The Clique firmly controlled university government, and he angered the Professor after he became principal.

As an avocation, the Maratha wrote fiction. In one story that he published in Marathi he related a fictional, but nonetheless autobiographical, incident that occurred while he was principal. In the incident a member of the Maharashtra Legislative Assembly, a coarse and rude man, approaches the principal of a college and demands that he admit the son of a friend to the college. The friend is very influential politically in the region, but the son is poorly qualified. The principal tells the legislator that he is rude and refuses to comply. The legislator becomes angry, asks him who he thinks he is to speak to him in that manner, and threatens "to have (the Professor) fail all your students." Supporters of the Professor threatened the Principal with legal action, but the case never materialized.

Rather than engage in a fight with the Clique, the Maratha resigned as principal. He returned to the university from which he had taken a leave of absence. It was from this position that he applied for the position of Head of the Mathematics Department on the postgraduate campus.

In June, 1984 the Executive Council approved an advertisement for a position to fill a distinguished chair as Head of the Department of Mathematics on the postgraduate campus. The position required a specialty that complied with that held by the Maratha and the outsider Brahman. They were equal in other ways as well. Each held the status of reader in his department. Each also applied successfully for outside research funds.

The Executive Council set up a selection committee comprising two outside experts, the Aspirant, who was an appointee of the Chancellor and the Vice-Chancellor. They were required to rank and recommend two names from the pool of applicants to the Executive Council that would then make the appointment. In January 1985 the committee recommended in order of preference the Maratha and the outsider Brahman. In blatant disregard of the recommendation, the Executive Council, which the Professor controlled, appointed a Brahman professor who had not even applied for the position but who was a supporter of the Professor. In so doing the Executive Council bent considerably the provisions of the University Act.

According to the Act a selection committee may recommend for appointment the names of "other persons who have not applied or appeared before it, and who are duly qualified." The Executive Council can only appoint such a person on the recommendation of the selection committee if it also justified its decisions in writing to the Chancellor. The Executive Council did not comply with either stipulation.

This action appeared to many people to be an abuse of Executive Council authority and many were upset at its action. Some members of the Executive Council who opposed the Clique also opposed the recommendation. All other Executive Councillors, including the Aspirant, supported the action.

The Maverick became a strong advocate of the Maratha. No one supported the second candidate, the outsider Brahman, as strongly. The Maverick sought legal counsel from the university's legal officer on behalf of the Maratha. In his opinion the legal counsel decided that the action of the Executive Council was illegal. The Maratha also received a sympathetic response from the Chancellor. This was because the Maratha's brother was a successful physician with friends and clientele among Maratha members of the legislature. He had them bring the issue to the Chancellor's attention because he was critical of the Clique. But the Chancellor was about to leave for another post overseas and could do nothing except express his sympathy. The Maratha wrote a long letter to the next Chancellor. In it he detailed the incident and the sense of the provision of the Act that supported his appointment.

Under these pressures, in June 1985 the Executive Council rescinded its recommendation. The issue again reverted to appointing one of the individuals on the original list. At the meeting in which a final decision was to be made, only seven members of the Executive Council attended. The vote was four to three in favour of appointing the Maratha. Those opposed included the Professor and two of his allies. Those who supported him included the Pro-VC of Episode Six who, in the absence of the VC, broke a tie vote.

The Professor complained to the new Chancellor that the vote should be set aside. However, events suggest that the Clique did not take this situation seriously. Considering how well it knew the provisions of the Act, it never attempted to justify why it nominated an individual that the selection committee did not recommend. Concerning the final vote that appointed the Maratha, the Aspirant said simply that it was unfortunate because the outsider Brahman had been a reader for a long period on the campus and deserved the promotion.

Once the issue was decided the Aspirant helped the

Maratha get accommodation on the campus. The Professor visited and congratulated him on the appointment. He asked for his political support. The Maratha thought the Professor's greeting was a magnanimous gesture. But he withheld his support.

III

Episode

College *Esprit de Corp*, or How Good Old Boys Treat an Outsider

This episode spanned seven years, from 1973 to 1980. It revolved around the promotion to professor of an outsider Brahman (hereafter the Protagonist) and attempts by Pune Brahmans to prohibit this for no better reason other than he was an outsider. The essence of the problem was that the promotion of the Protagonist to professor could have resulted in his becoming Director of the Deccan College, a constituent institution of Poona University. This was unacceptable to Pune Brahmans who were the college's alumni and staffed the Deccan Educational Society who managed it and valued it highly.

The first Director of Deccan College, Professor H. D. Sankalia, was involved in this episode and described some of it in detail in his autobiography (Sankalia 1978). Although he was not always friendly toward the Protagonist, he decried and condemned the extent to which caste interests superseded considerations of merit in denying the Protagonist the professorship. The episode reveals the conflict engendered by the contradiction in caste, institution, and region the significance for individuals involved in the fight of the symbolic potency of the Deccan College, and the value placed on it by Pune Brahmans. To understand the intricacy of the alignment of agents from the university and state government who got involved in the issue, we must begin with the inception of the Deccan College.

The Deccan College was established in 1821 and attained a venerable status. The British closed it in 1932 because of the expense of operating it. This offended its Past Student Association which was comprised almost exclusively of Pune Brahmans. They went to court to have it reopened. In 1938 the court decided in their favour and it reopened as a postgraduate research institution affiliated to another university. In 1939 the Department of Archaeology, the focus of attention here, was created. The management of the college hired Sankalia, a non-Brahman outsider, in a dual capacity: As Head of the Department of Archaeology and Director of the Deccan College. At that time India did not have many qualified archaeologists and Sankalia gradually was assimilated over the years as a Pune Brahman. He became an internationally recognized scholar, fiercely loyal to the Deccan College and, for a number or years, antagonistic to the Protagonist.

When Poona University was established in 1949, the Deccan College became one of its constituent institutions. In 1958 the UGC approved a proposal submitted by Sankalia and awarded a special grant-in-aid to the university to develop the Deccan College Department of Archaeology further. Through a series of complicated and now somewhat vague events, political agents on the postgraduate campus used this grant to establish a duplicate department on the postgraduate campus. This was unusual, for it was not common at that time for city college Brahmans, who were in charge on the campus to use a grant for the development of a city college to develop the postgraduate campus. I shall refer to this department as the University Archaeology Department. The result was that the university now had two Archaeology Departments that nearly duplicated each other. The Deccan College management, including Sankalia, immediately perceived the development of the university's Archaeology Department as a threat to the integrity of the Deccan College department. Much of the subsequent fighting can be understood as an attempt by Deccan College authorities to squash the university's department.

For the next four years Sankalia managed to freeze the development of the university department and worked hard to develop the Deccan College department. He insured the construction of buildings and facilities in the Deccan College and hired faculty. Almost all of his hires were Pune Brahmans, some of whom had been his students. However, in 1962 the Protagonist, also a student of Sankalia, was hired as a lecturer in the University's Archaeology Department. For a few years he was its only faculty member. Subsequently he managed to hire additional faculty and staff for the university department. As senior member of the department, he was appointed reader in 1968 and became head of the university department. Sankalia viewed this as an ominous event.

Technically the Deccan College Archaeology Department was subordinate to the university department because the Deccan College was a constituent institution of Poona University and subordinate to the postgraduate campus. Additionally, should promotions and appointments fall properly, the head of the university department could easily become the next director of the Deccan College. Sankalia feared that he might absorb the Deccan College department into the university department. Although Sankalia liked the Protagonist well enough and recognized him to be an exceptional scholar, he also was wary of him getting too much power. In part, Sankalia's stature and the domination of the university by city college Brahmans were sufficient to thwart any plans the Protagonist had for developing the university department. The Protagonist's status also worked against any intentions he had to develop the university department. He was junior to another reader in the Deccan College department who shared his archaeological speciality and who had been hired by Sankalia. He was more or less contemporary in hiring status with at least two other individuals who also held the ranks of readers in the Deccan College department. Their wishes and intentions received priority over the Protagonist's.

In 1972 as a result of the Protagonist's efforts the UGC recognized the university department to be worthy of special financial assistance. This placed additional strain on the relationship between the Protagonist and Sankalia; the award elevated the university department's status considerably. It upset Sankalia and he requested the Protagonist, as head of the university department, to reject the funds. He, of course, refused and differences between the two escalated.

Events in 1972 that are discussed in Chapter 5 forced the state government to replace the Vice-Chancellor and Executive Council. This compounded the differences between Sankalia and the Protagonist. Sankalia was among those individuals the Chancellor appointed to the reconstituted Executive Council. He took advantage of this position to have the Executive Council approve a new position of professor in the Deccan College department. It was an important position as the person who occupied it would become the next director of the Deccan College when Sankalia retired, which he did in 1973.

The Protagonist applied for the position. The selection committee awarded it to the reader in the Deccan College who was senior to the Protagonist and shared his speciality. This happened because the reader was close to Sankalia and favoured by the Deccan College management which was able to muster considerable support on the Executive Council. The Protagonist remained head of the university department.

Following the initiation of the 1974 Poona University Act that restructured university government, the Chancellor appointed a Pune Brahman as Vice-Chancellor of the university. In the subsequent elections to fill the offices of university government the Gang and CC Leader regained the seats on the Executive Council that they held before the events of 1972. But members of the Clique also acquired seats on the council and they began to challenge the Gang's power and influence. In general, in this episode the Clique supported the Protagonist and the Gang opposed him. Subsequent events related to allocating and filling positions in the Deccan College Archaeology Department and university department resulted in one more conflict between these teams.

Shortly after the elections, the Executive Council, led by the Clique, requested a position of professor from the UGC for the university department.[1] This position was described to fit the speciality of the Protagonist. With no malice apparently intended the UGC approved the position as described but omitted a critical adjective that sharply defined the Protagonist's specialty. This rendered the description of the position ambiguous. The new director immediately lobbied the Executive Council to have the position approved for the Deccan College department. The Protagonist claims that the director also told him to his face in a heated discussion over the matter that "Pune Brahmans would band together to keep him from getting the appointment." The Vice-Chancellor appointed a committee to advise him on the matter. It recommended that the position remain in the university department and comply with the Protagonist's specialty.

Still, the director and others from the Deccan College

successfully delayed the approval of the position in the university department and over the next couple years lobbied to move the position to the Deccan College. Ultimately, the position was moved. After that, the Deccan lobby garnered sufficient support on the Executive Council to advertise the position in either of two specializations. One fitted both the Protagonist and the Director and the other a reader in the Deccan College department. The Executive Council also reserved the right to make an appointment in either specialization.

Subsequent events revealed that the strategy behind this move was to describe sufficient specialities so that one of the favourites of the Deccan College Management and Director could qualify and receive the appointment. This would preclude the appointment of the Protagonist, for whoever the committee selected for the position would become the next director of the Deccan College when the current director retired. He was required by university rules to do so in 1980.

When the advertisement for the position appeared in early 1977, four people applied: the Protagonist and three individuals from the Deccan College, two of whom were the readers who were close in status to the Protagonist. We shall call them candidates A and B. The third candidate, C, was the director of the Deccan College. Recall that he was senior to the Protagonist and shared his academic and research specialities.

The Executive Council asked the retired director, Sankalia, to compile the panel of experts to interview and recommend candidates to fill the position. But the panel he submitted was somehow altered radically. The panel that the Executive Council convened had no experts in either of the specialities under consideration. Nevertheless, it recommended either candidate A or candidate C for the first speciality, the one for which the Protagonist was qualified, and candidate A again for the second. It was obvious that despite whichever speciality filled the position, the Protagonist was excluded.

By this time the Aspirant, a leader of the Clique, was actively involved in the matter on behalf of the Protagonist. Nonetheless, after several months of debate, in October, 1977, the Executive Council approved the appointment of candidate C, the director, for the specialty that fitted the Protagonist. He immediately declined the position and a representative of the Gang on the Executive Council moved for the appointment of candidate A. Confronted with anger by the Protagonist's supporters – the Clique, some bureaucrats in state government, and now Sankalia – the Executive Council ultimately refused to make any appointment.

This manipulation of caste at the expense of merit outraged Sankalia. He now added a section to his 1978 autobiography that condemned the politics behind the selection. He concluded, "When I saw all these things happening before my own eyes, I literally wept, not because the department, which had been developed from nothing was being torn into pieces, but because for exercising authority all the worst aspects of human nature had gained ascendancy." (Sankalia 1978:147)

In December 1978, when the Clique assumed control of university government the Executive Council obtained another professor position and advertised it in the speciality that fitted the qualification of the Protagonist. In early 1979 the state secretary of education intervened. He was a good friend of the CC Leader and the Gang. He announced that if the university tried to make the appointment, the state government would withhold funds to support the position. In addition, he informed the Vice-Chancellor and Executive

Council that the university department was to be merged with the Deccan College department. The state education minister and his supporters lobbied behind the scenes to accomplish this merger.

While all this was going on the Deccan College department filled six teaching positions in quick order. The positions were sanctioned by the UGC in July 1979 and advertised in November. Interviews were held on February 8, 1980. Selections were approved on February 17. Letters of offer were issued between the 18 and 20 and candidates were appointed immediately upon their acceptance. One of the appointments at the level of professor was awarded to candidate A whose name had appeared on each list recommended to the Executive Council in 1978. Later that year he became the new director of the Deccan College.

The Protagonist was upset and wrote a letter to the Chancellor. He lamented that after 19 years of uninterrupted and exemplary service to the university, "All the important people in the University, leading (scholars) in the country and even the chairman of the UGC, are aware of the injustice done and being done to me and they all wonder what is the meaning of university autonomy if the state government can prevent the university from filling a post for which it has committed money simply because (an outsider) like me stands the possibility of being appointed to it" (Parenthesis added to protect identities).

Even prior to this letter the Protagonist had sought support from the state government, but with little success. Individuals in state government who were sympathetic to his problem also were outsiders and low in status, largely assistants to ministers of the legislative assembly. Because of that they could not do much. Unless one of the ministers was allied to one of the involved parties, as the one minister was to the Gang, the issue was not big enough to warrant their attention.

Gradually however, the Clique, a mix of Pune and outsider Brahmans, Marathas and other non-Brahmans, was able to get the upper hand in this matter. In 1978 the state government changed and the Clique had better friends in this government. It did not attempt to undo the appointment of the six individuals in the Deccan College department or the merging of the university department with it. But it did finally procure the position that the State Secretary of Education had denied earlier. That was awarded to the Protagonist in 1980 and he became a professor. By this time, because of the merger, he held a position in the Deccan College department, albeit uncomfortably, given his colleagues. When I attempted to find out how he interpreted the support he had received from the Clique in obtaining the position, I asked him if he knew the caste of those who had helped him. He responded, "Why, they were Brahmans on the postgraduate campus!" He was not aware that much of his support had come from non-Brahmans, in particular the Aspirant, a CKP.

The Protagonist did not become director of the Deccan College at this time. But moves were already afoot to establish the Deccan College as a separate university. In 1989 the Aspirant became the Vice-Chancellor of Poona University. With his help the Protagonist became, in 1996, the first Vice-Chancellor of the new "deemed-to-be" university, the Deccan College Postgraduate and Research Institute.

Note

1. In Indian universities an individual is not promoted on the basis of merit to a higher position, such as from lecturer to reader to professor. A higher position must exist in the department before an individual can occupy it. This is enabled

by the retirement or death of an incumbent, or the creation of a new position. This is similar to the British system of higher education.

IV

Episode

Vengeance is Mine, Sayeth Whoever Sits in Power

This episode is one of the university's more notorious instances of covert political intrigue, conflict related to caste contradictions and the involvement of agents external to the university. It concerns a department head that ran afoul of his department and the Clique. At one point forces opposed to him rallied on the basis of the anti-Brahman ideology that remains alive and well among Marathas who represent sugar factories and their lobby in the state's rural areas (Baviskar 1980; Attwood 1992). Although this episode involves a series of seemingly disparate events, an intricate and complex caste and political agency was at work. The episode lasted from about 1979 to 1981, but it began several years before.

The Head, as I shall refer to him, was a Karhada or Maharashtra Brahman. He was born and raised in a Marathi-speaking community outside the state on one of its border areas. He came to the Anthropology Department at Poona University in 1960 with a Masters degree from another university and claimed later that he had received a Ph D from that university. By the time his problems began, no one questioned his credentials. He had been in the university for a long time and spoke Marathi, and local Brahmans accepted him as one of their own.

In the early 1960s the Anthropology Department was a component of the Sociology Department. He was one of three individuals who were hired at about the same time in the anthropology component. I shall refer to his colleagues as A and B. By the mid 1970s it was clear that anthropology and sociology would separate. By the time that occurred in 1977 four other individuals, each of whom had been a student of the Head, had been hired in anthropology department. However, by this time A and B had lost their jobs. Rumours on campus held that the Head was behind these dismissals to insure that he would become Head of the Anthropology Department when it became autonomous.

The Head, with the help of B, charged A with having sex with a student. Based on this accusation the university fired A on a charge of immorality. Some thought the punishment was excessive because A and the student intended to get married and later did. The Head then enlisted the help of the other four teachers to have B dismissed on charges of intimidating students to bring charges of immorality against A! As the senior faculty and only reader in the Anthropology Department, he became its head when it separated from sociology in 1977.

An indication that the Head was in trouble surfaced in June, 1978. The Vice-Chancellor, the first and, so far, only Maratha to hold that office, received an anonymous letter that listed 12 counts of "academic fraud" attributed to the Head. The letter questioned his scholarly competence, the legitimacy of his Ph D, and accused him of chicanery in attaining the status of reader. After receiving the letter the Vice-Chancellor convened a meeting with members of the Anthropology Department to investigate the matter. All four teachers supported the Head and denied knowledge of the letter. The author of the letter remains a mystery.

Following this incident intra-departmental squabbling began between the Head and the four teachers. One teacher was an ambitious outsider Brahman (from now on the Outsider). He had a Ph D and was the Head's favourite. But at this time he began to have difficulties with the Head. Soon another teacher replaced him as the Head's favourite. He too was an outsider Brahman and also had a Ph D. The Outsider and two remaining teachers, who were Pune Brahmans but held Masters degrees only, began to complain that the Head was increasingly tyrannical, and they, especially the Outsider, began to feel threatened by him. A rumour started to circulate that the Outsider had sent the anonymous letter. In 1978, around the time all this was transpiring the Outsider and his colleague's moved files and other information out of the department office. They used this information to document a case of financial fraud and overbearing comportment against the Head. During this time other events were occurring which make this documentation especially significant.

The Outsider had been talking to members of the Clique about his problems with the Head. These included, among others, the Protagonist and Aspirant (see Episode Three) and the Maratha who soon would become Vice-Chancellor. At this time he was a member of the Executive Council. It was natural that the Outsider would eventually make contact with the Clique. He was one among many outsider Brahmans who claimed that Pune Brahmans were oppressing them, and the Clique took advantage of this. One way the Clique, especially the Aspirant, recruited support was by helping outsider Brahmans, such as the Protagonist of Episode Three, when they had problems with Pune Brahmans. Because of this, even before securing control of university government, the Clique was aware of the Outsider's concerns regarding the Head. And the Clique had its own complaint against the Head.

In 1979 the Head incurred the Clique's antagonism. As we

saw in Chapter 6, after the Maratha was appointed Vice-Chancellor in 1978 the Campus Leader, one of the leaders of the Clique, lost his chance to be appointed Vice-Chancellor. In the elections which followed the appointment of the Maratha as Vice-Chancellor, the Campus Leader solicited help for election to the Executive Council. The Head was a friend of his opponent for the seat on the Executive Council, and he had not been silent about his dislike of the Campus Leader. It was not difficult for the Campus Leader to identify the Head as one who had opposed him. Many believe that after this he orchestrated the actions by which the Clique and the Maratha Vice-Chancellor victimized the Head.

In August 1979 the Outsider and his colleagues in the Anthropology Department presented the charges they had documented against the Head to the Maratha Vice-Chancellor. He appointed a retired judge to review the charges. In March, 1980, his report exonerated the Head. It cited the weakness of the charges and the lack of evidence to support the allegations. He did admonish the Head to be more diplomatic and democratic in his relations with his faculty.

The Head was not pleased with these events. Although he was not certain how the information was procured, he blamed the Student Administrative Assistant for helping the teachers. The assistant was a Maratha and was appointed some time before. In July, 1980, when the assistant's probationary period of appointment ended, the Head terminated him on charges of presenting a false medical certificate to take. Prior to the assistant's dismissal, the Outsider had begun to curry his favour. He was flattered by the Outsider's attention and sought help from him after he was terminated.

By this time the fear the Outsider and his two colleagues had of the Head was palpable. The Outsider claimed later that the brakes on his two-wheeler had been tampered with, and that the Head had hired a tribal *shaman* to bewitch him. He helped the student compile another, more incriminating list of charges. These charged the Head with fraudulent behaviour and financial irregularities. The student claimed that he observed these irregularities when he was Administrative Assistant.

In August 1980 the student sent the list of charges to the Chancellor, the Chief Minister of Maharashtra, all members of the Executive Council and Senate, the President and Secretary of the Teacher's Union, Heads of all Anthropology Departments in India, and to the Head himself. The President of the Teacher's Union formally presented the charges to the Maratha Vice-Chancellor for consideration. He had been asked to do this by the Outsider and the Aspirant. Since the charges appeared to be just, the Vice-Chancellor complied with their request to establish an inquiry committee to investigate the dismissal of the Administrative Assistant. The formation and composition of this committee is instructive.

At the request of the Vice-Chancellor, the Outsider initiated the formation of the inquiry committee. This was a clear sign that the Outsider was now an acceptable member of the Clique. He contacted the Administrative Assistant's eldest brother, a Maratha and officer in a rural sugar factory. The assistant's brother procured a list of previous members of the university's Executive Council from a previous member, a Maratha, who was the Principal of a college supported by another sugar factory. He and the Outsider then used the list to seek potential members for the committee.

The final culling of names resulted in several individuals, primarily Marathas, who were convinced that the Administrative Assistant was a victim of Brahman arrogance.

Among this group was another brother of the assistant. His wife's uncle was an ex-education minister in the state government. He was very influential and shared mutual friends and close acquaintances with the Maratha Vice-Chancellor. He contacted the Vice-Chancellor on the matter and they decided to name a three-man committee to hear the case. It comprised two Marathas and a Pune Brahman from a city college who, as we saw in Chapter 7, directed the agitation by the RSS[1] on campus in 1988-1989 and became Pro-Vice Chancellor of the university for a brief period in 1987-1988. He was thought to be an appropriate member of the committee because he was from the Administrative Assistant's native place and knew his family well. Of course, being a Brahman also gave additional credibility to the committee.

The Executive Council approved the appointment of the committee and charged it to investigate the case. In December 1980 the committee ruled in favour of reinstating the Administrative Assistant, and this was done. But the committee went beyond what most people understood to be their charge. They recommended another investigation of the Head based on the allegations in the charge sheet. The Executive Council appointed them to conduct it. In early 1981 they recommended to the Executive Council, which was dominated at the time by the Clique, that the Head be fired. And he was. They never gave him a chance to defend himself.

The action shocked a great many people. Most agreed that it was orchestrated by the Campus Leader in revenge for the Head's failure to support him in the 1979 election. Most people also thought that the punishment was excessive. The department's teachers, including the Outsider, claim they opposed firing the Head (some disagree with this). Campus department heads met and debated the issue. Although the Protagonist from Episode Three argued strongly to sustain the dismissal, most heads favoured his reinstatement. Their motives varied. Some were his friends. Others believed that he had been unjustly victimized by the Clique and Campus Leader. Some felt vulnerable. They believed that if he could be removed on such charges, so might they. As one said, "He was charged with what all of us do to run our departments. All of us could be found guilty of such charges."

The majority of the heads filed a petition with the Chancellor that pleaded for his reinstatement. Local newspapers wrote editorials on his behalf. The Head also mobilized his own support. His brother was well in with the Chief Minister of Maharashtra. He got the ear of the Chief Minister who pleaded his case with the Chancellor. Six months later the Executive Council reappointed him as a teacher, but not as Head of the Anthropology Department, and awarded him back pay.

Full restitution came to the Head in the early 1990s. In 1989 the Aspirant, who had worked to destroy the Head, became Vice-Chancellor. In 1993 university administration established a new programme of Health Sciences on campus. One of the Head's specialities was Medical Anthropology. The Vice-Chancellor appointed him director of the programme.

Notes

1. As noted elsewhere, the RSS, sometimes the RSSS (Rashtriya Swayam Sevak Sangh, or Volunteers in Service to the Nation) is a conservative Hindu fundamentalist political association. Its involvement in the university's politics was discussed in Chapter 7.

V

Episode
The Name of the Game is Research, isn't it?

The events of this episode involved an American scholar who was instrumental in the university acquiring a large research grant. She got sucked into the fight by those who were either attempting to remove the Campus Leader from the university's politics, discredit the Clique, or get some piece of the grant's action. This episode reveals in some detail how the aggressiveness and independent actions of the Campus Leader antagonized his opponents and also disturbed and embarrassed the Clique. The episode also reveals the intricacy and extent of tactics political agents employed to achieve their ends. The events took place in 1985 and 1986. But to understand the episode it is necessary to begin several years before.

In the late 1960s the Campus Leader, a Pune Brahman who was dedicated to the postgraduate campus, was trying to establish five interdisciplinary programs – he called them schools – on the postgraduate campus. They were intended to promote the development of India. By 1979 the Campus Leader's ambition to become either Vice-Chancellor or an Executive Councillor of the university had been dashed. But he was successful in obtaining modest funds from the UGC to initiate the schools. Members of the Clique became their directors or were otherwise involved. The Maratha Vice-Chancellor, his protégé, appointed him director of the school of his choice, the Educational Media Research Centre (EMRC, as noted elsewhere). He continued in this position after his retirement in the early 1980s at what many believed was an excessive salary.

Besides the funds he received from the UGC to support the schools, the Campus Leader managed to obtain additional funds and equipment for the EMRC. His enemies alleged loudly that these funds came out of budgets and grants to departments that did not support him in the 1979 elections (see Chapter 6). Others complained that he managed to finesse equipment meant for other departments. Both were true.

In one instance the head of a department made arrangements with an American agency to receive a number of surplus typewriters for his department. But he had run afoul of the Campus Leader. When the Campus Leader heard that the representatives of the agency were on campus he hosted a dinner function for them. The typewriters ended up in the EMRC.

In 1978, on a trip to the United States the Campus Leader met a professor of Communications at Cornell University (SW hereafter). She had an interest in India. The Campus Leader impressed her with his explanation of a project regarding how Indian development could be promoted through the interdisciplinary schools and the use of video technologies. She gave the Campus Leader copies of her publications and grant proposals that she thought might be helpful to the project.

A year or so later, in an attempt to seek funds for the EMRC, the Campus Leader circulated a booklet worldwide to various departments that described his project. Eventually it came to the attention of SW. The booklet did not represent the project as SW understood it from their previous meeting. But it drew freely, frequently verbatim and without citation, from her publications and proposals. To sate her curiosity SW made a trip to Poona University in 1982. After talking to the Campus Leader she returned with little expectation that the project would be implemented. She underestimated the Campus Leader's skill and tenacity.

In the fall of 1983 SW received a research proposal from the international section of the National Science Foundation (NSF). The Campus Leader submitted it to obtain support for a development project through the EMRC. The proposal referred to American scholars and universities as though the Campus Leader had extensive contact with them, and he listed SW and Cornell University as the American affiliates for the research. The proposal was not acceptable to NSF as it was written. Still, it impressed reviewers enough that NSF requested SW to render it acceptable for funding through PL 480 rupees.[1] By this time two members of the Clique were at a small American university to which the Clique had a conduit through an old member who had emigrated (this institutional relationship was discussed in Chapter 7). They contacted SW and requested her to keep them informed of the progress of the proposal and to write them into it in some capacity that would provide them with funds. SW was somewhat amused by all this.

SW got together with four old friends, two from Cornell University Departments and two other communications professors from other universities. Each was an expert in the field of communications, had an international reputation and was interested in the development of India. They reworked the proposal and in November returned it to NSF.[2] It contained a budget of six million rupees that was to be expended in phases over a five year period.

In January 1984, SW made a second trip to India. She was

concerned because she and Cornell were now identified with the proposal. She wanted to insure that in the event NSF funded the proposal Poona University was committed and capable of handling it. She also wanted the project to have a local director with the qualifications that were established in the proposal. The Vice-Chancellor, the Campus Leader, and other members of the Clique received her and assured her that all would be well. She also met other people on the campus who treated her very graciously and with whom she spoke openly about the project. SW thought their interest was merely a continuation of the reception she was receiving. She did not know they were part of a cabal opposed to the Campus Leader and Clique.

In March 1984, NSF reviewers accepted the proposal but said it belonged in a different agency. In August, 1984, with help from NSF, the Office on International Cooperation and Development within the United States Department of Agriculture (USDA) agreed to fund it with PL 480 rupees. In November 1984, 1.7 million rupees were transferred to Poone University. SW was the principal investigator.

In the months between SW's second visit and the award of the grant, the Vice-Chancellor appointed the Campus Leader as the director of the research project. This was in addition to his position as director of the EMRC. The appointment included a salary drawn against the grant that was even higher than his EMRC salary. He also established an advisory committee for the project that was comprised primarily of members of the Clique, none of whom were sufficiently qualified for such a position. Once the funds were awarded rumours of their misuse, nepotism and assorted corruption became rampant and implicated the Campus Leader.

The most extreme allegation was that he put the funds into a private bank account and either shared the interest with the bank manager or a relative, or used them for personal desiderata. Some argue it was all of the above. He suddenly appeared in a new, bright red Maruti car. He claimed that it was necessary for the project. He flew frequently to Delhi, presumably to discuss the project with the USDA. Opponents considered these trips to be junkets. Sometimes he used the project's funds to support other projects in the EMRC, such as purchasing equipment and providing funds to friends in the EMRC who he said were conducting research, but not necessarily on the project. He saw nothing undue in all this. From his perspective all the programs and departments subsumed under the EMRC comprised one large enterprise and financial pool. This was simply the way he always operated in the university, to the frequent consternation of friends and foes alike. The Clique tried to check his ambitions. Foes were always out to get him.

In January 1985, SW returned to India. She had been alerted to alleged indiscretions by the Campus Leader. Contentions between her and the Clique were immediate. It took more than two weeks for the Vice-Chancellor to convene the project's advisory board. She was upset at the misunderstanding of the project, the indiscriminate use of funds, and the appointment of an unqualified research director, a member of the Clique of course. To rectify the situation she insisted on the appointment of a board that was more compatible with the project goals and a project director with the qualifications specified in the proposal and with whom she could work. She threatened to withdraw the grant if proposal guidelines were not adhered to. The Vice-Chancellor finally took action to appoint a new local project director.

The Outsider, the ambitious Brahman of Episode Two, whom she had met by this time, was selected as the most qualified to be the local project director. He also related well to SW and the US researchers who helped to design the grant for NSF and came to Pune as consultants and research personnel. However, by this time other events related to the EMRC were converging with SW's problems over control of the USDA grant. Individuals opposed to the Campus Leader hatched a plan to bring him to ruin, and SW was its *modus operandi*.

In January, 1985, around the time SW arrived, a Canadian consultant prepared a report on the EMRC as part of an obligation for participating in a two week workshop held in the EMRC. He submitted it to the Vice-Chancellor, the Campus Leader (as director of the EMRC), a member of the UGC and other individuals who were associated in some way with the EMRC. Between the reports opening remarks that were conciliatory and its conclusions that were meant to be constructive 27 pages were extremely critical of the EMRC and the Campus Leader. Coincidentally, the fury surrounding the appointment of the first Pro-VC erupted at this time (See Episode Six). The involvement of the Campus Leader in the attempts to discredit the first Pro-VC was big news in the local press. This, coupled with the new disclosures in the consultant's report, led those who opposed the Campus Leader, such as the Brahman lobby, to consider an auspicious time to depose him. The report was the catalyst around which the opposition to the Campus Leader began to mobilize.

The Vice-Chancellor tried to have the report reviewed quietly in the Executive Council. Opponents to the Clique and Campus Leader made it an issue and a quiet review impossible. By April, when the first Pro-VC was appointed, it had been published in part in the press and discussed editorially in various local newspapers, all of which were extremely critical of the Clique and Campus Leader. The Vice-Chancellor had little choice other than to appoint a committee to review the report's allegations. The committee included a member of the UGC and two respected individuals who were not associated with the university.

In addition, six department heads, each a Brahman (except, nominally, the Maverick) with a historically grounded grudge against the Campus Leader, also decided to try to depose him. Three or four of these individuals met SW on her visit to the university in January 1984. They were, in part, genuinely interested in the possibility of a large research project coming to the university; it would be a coup that would add to the university's prestige. A couple also hoped to become the project's director, for the amount of rupees involved and its considerable perks, such as foreign travel and additional salary, were well known. SW claims that she had no idea that this was the formation of a cabal against the Campus Leader.

In early May 1985, according to SW, one of the cabal's instigators brought his friend, a reporter from a local newspaper, to meet her and "learn more" about the USDA project. She agreed and met informally with them for an hour. SW says that she did not think much about the interview and that the reporter was casual in the discussion and did not take notes. A few days later the interview appeared in the paper. It was a scathing denunciation of the Campus Leader, his scholarship, integrity, honesty, and character. SW was cited as the source of the attack, as well as blatant statements that she deplored his association with the research project. SW insisted that she did not make the comments and claimed that she had been used by others in their vendetta against the Campus Leader. Others in the cabal say that she was a willing and avid participant.

Despite the investigation of the inquiry committee and the attack on the Campus Leader by the cabal, nothing came of it. The Clique's power on campus buffered the attacks. Nonetheless, for several months relations among those who were involved in the project were tense. People in and outside the university called for the Campus Leader's resignation and measures to curb the power of the Clique. In August, 1985, the UGC presented a long report on the issues raised by the Canadian expert's report. It admonished the Campus Leader to be more prudent in his activities. The Outsider and SW gradually began to implement the project.

The sharpest fallout from the episode affected SW. Because of several delays in obtaining a visa she did not return to India until the following January 1986 instead of September 1985. The university administration, synonymously the Clique, claimed publicly that it was doing all it could to hasten her return and that the delay was due to unfortunate bureaucratic problems. The private flow of information on the campus told of the Clique's bitterness regarding the interview and its considerable efforts to impede her return to Poona University.

Notes

1. Public Law 480 provided for rupees that the United States acquired through trade with India to be set aside and used for, among other things, research by American scholars in India. The law is now defunct.
2. Two of them told me that they did not take the task very seriously. The final product was a result of some brainstorming, considerable conviviality, and a wish by a couple to be able to go to India as consultants to the project. As one claimed, it would be hard to know exactly what the proposed research was supposed to accomplish, and they were surprised that the proposal was funded. The lack of methodology did hamper and delay seriously its implementation. However, once this was worked out in the field the project did accomplish its goals successfully.

VI

Episode

The Case of the Recalcitrant VC and the Reluctant Pro-VC

In the absence of the Vice-Chancellor, or in the event he is unable to perform his duties, the Act empowers a Pro-Vice - Chancellor to exercise the authority of the Vice-Chancellor's office. The appointment of Pune University's first Pro-Vice-Chancellor in 1985 resulted in the first open conflict between the Clique and the extant Vice-Chancellor (1984-1989), or VC, as I refer to him.

The decision by the VC to offer this appointment to a principal from a city college without approval of the Clique evoked new and old contradictions in the university and presaged events to come. They are explored fully in Chapter 7. By 1985 the institutional contradiction between the postgraduate campus and city colleges appeared to have been resolved in favour of the campus. But it re-emerged. For the first time the postgraduate campus was subjected to "politicization", that is, the intrusion of outside political interests into university affairs. Contradictory ideologies and symbols related to caste and politics charged the environment.

During the VC's first year in office in 1985 the Executive Council, which was controlled by the Clique, considered seriously the desirability of appointing a Pro-Vice-Chancellor to assist him. The Executive Council, more than the VC, argued the need to appoint a Pro-VC. Officially the Executive Council said that it sought a Pro-VC because the tasks of the VC were increasingly burdensome and he needed assistance. Unofficially it was because the Clique wanted someone in the office who could be groomed to be the next Vice-Chancellor and to insure better control of the current VC. He was resisting increasingly his subordination to the Clique, especially the Professor who at that time was the most powerful person in the university. Some members of the Clique had an interest in occupying the office of Pro-Vice-Chancellor. Some of them saw that office as a stepping stone to the office of Vice-Chancellor. Others saw it as a source of influence in university government that they sought to control.

In early 1985 the Executive Council forwarded a slate of three names comprising members of the Clique, each a non-Brahman, to the Chancellor for his consideration to approve a Pro-VC. The Chancellor had appointed the current VC and was antagonistic to the Clique. He rejected the slate and instructed the VC and Executive Council to seek someone from outside the Clique. In March 1985, without discussing the matter either with the Clique or Executive Council, the VC called the Principal of Pune Law College and offered him the position. It is not clear how the VC arrived at this decision. But the motivation behind the offer became coherent in terms of his political project as it evolved. Subsequent events suggest that it was an attempt by the VC to assert his independence from the Clique. (The VC's project was discussed in Chapter 7.) The Chancellor accepted the Principal and appointed him Pro-VC.

On the surface the VC argued that the Principal was the best man for the job. Beneath that, other considerations influenced his decision. Politically it was an act of rebellion. He wanted an ally, a buffer against the increasing domination of the Clique and the loss of his influence in university government. Functionally he wanted a person to whom he could delegate some matters that he wanted to avoid, such as voting on appointments and promotions supported by the Clique with which he disagreed. This relieved him of any association with controversial actions. It also allowed him to maintain his independence, at least symbolically, from the Clique and not tarnish his reputation unduly. He also hoped that the Pro-VC could represent him in some of the more delicate aspects of the university's government, such as matters related to corruption by the Clique.

The Clique was upset. Not only had the VC for the first time acted independently of it on a major issue, the Principal was totally unacceptable to it. He symbolized the city colleges and their Pune Brahman organization, for he was a Chitpavan Brahman. This alone would have been sufficient to make the Clique uneasy. But he also was a liberal, a humanist, a socialist, a highly respected legal scholar, and very outspoken on social, political and university issues, including the corruption by the Clique in university government. He also was vocal in opposition to the Congress Party after the declaration of the Emergency by Indira Gandhi and Hindu fundamentalists who had considerable influence in the city and its colleges through the RSS.

Upon receiving the offer the Principal told the VC that he wanted to think about it. Almost immediately forces began to align to support or oppose his appointment. Support came from on and off the campus from reputed Pune Brahmans, the Brahman Lobby as it was called, and the local press. Students organized to solicit names on a petition to support the Principal. There was hope (as there had been before) among his supporters that the Principal could neutralize the influence and power of the Clique.

Although the Principal had enemies among politicians,

professional lawyers and others in the city who opposed his liberal views, the Clique provided the major opposition to his appointment. It responded immediately to the VC's action and quickly made him aware of its displeasure. Not only did it exert pressure on the VC to withdraw the offer, it – some say the Campus Leader – mobilized student political associations that belonged to the right wing Bharatiya Janata Party (BJP) and the RSS to demonstrate against the appointment. The Campus Leader called the Principal and urged him to withdraw. Even the VC had second thoughts about the appointment. He was under extreme pressure from the Clique, especially the Campus Leader, who was an old and dear friend (a relationship that was explored in Chapter 7) and was upset with the way the events had turned.

The situation became so tense that at one point the VC called the Principal and suggested that, perhaps, under the circumstances, he ought to decline the position. The VC also offered unconvincingly to resign (it was refused by the Chancellor). In part this was an act of defence against the Clique. In part it was designed to save his reputation. At this point the Clique, even his friend the Campus Leader, was willing to accept his resignation because, by statute, the Pro-Vice-Chancellor must quit his office when the Vice-Chancellor quits. But opponents to the Clique on the campus and notable Pune Brahmans encouraged the Principal not to back down.

About this time, in a strong show of support, about 140 people, mainly prominent Pune Brahmans and others from the postgraduate campus, convened in a hotel and rallied for the Principal. Representatives from this group met the VC on his behalf. A local newspaper wrote a long editorial on the matter. It implicated by innuendo various members of the Clique, condemned their role in the student protests, announced that a student organization had threatened the Principal and encouraged support of the VC. On advice from his friends, and because he didn't want to appear to buckle under pressure from political agitators, the Principal accepted the position. The Campus Leader called the Principal and congratulated him.

To finally clarify the situation, the Principal requested a private meeting with the VC. When he arrived the Campus Leader was also present. The Principal was upset and told the VC that he had requested a private meeting. The VC responded that "the (Campus Leader) is closer to me than my wife". There are conflicting stories about what transpired at this meeting. Some say that the three of them struck a deal. They deny it. Regardless, the Principal served as Pro-VC for exactly one year to the day. Then he resigned to accept a UGC Fellowship. Shortly after that the Executive Council approved the appointment as Pro-VC of another Pune Brahman who had been a Principal of Fergusson College. He was acceptable to the Clique because he was elderly, not a threat and not well liked in the city colleges. He also would not be much of an ally for the VC, and, because he was a Pune Brahman, the Clique could claim neutrality in its caste biases.

References Cited

Andersen, Walter K. and Shridhar D. Damle, *The Brotherhood in Saffron: The Rashtriya Swayamsevak Sangh and Hindu Revivalism* (New Delhi: Vistaar Publications, 1987)

Attwood, Donald W., *Raising Cane: The Political Economy of Sugar in Western India*, (Boulder: Westview Press,1992)

Baviskar, B.S., *The Politics of Development: Sugar Cooperatives in Rural Maharashtra*, (Delhi: Oxford University Press,1992)

Bhoite, U.B., *Sociology of Indian Intellectuals*, (Jaipur: Rawat Publications, 1987)

Callincos, Alex, *Making History: Agency, Structure and Change in Social Theory*, (Ithaca, NY: Cornell University Press,1988)

Carter, Anthony T., *Elite Politics in Rural India: Political Stratification and Political Alliances in Western India*, (London: Cambridge University Press,1974)

Cashman, Richard I., *The Myth of the Lokamanya: Tilak and Mass Politics in Maharashtra*, (Berkeley: University of California Press,1975)

Contursi, Janet A., Militant Hindus and Buddhist Dalits: Hegemony and Resistance in an India Slum, *American Ethnologist* 16(3):441-457,1989

Duff, James Grant. [1863]. *History of the Marathas, Volume I*, (Delhi: Low Price Publications,1974)

Gokhale, Balkrishna Govind, *Poona in the Eighteenth Center: An Urban History*, (Delhi: Oxford University Press,1988)

Golay, W. H., *The University of Ponna: 1949-1974*, (Poona: University of Poona Press, 1974)

Gore, M. S., *Non-Brahman Movements in Maharashtra*, (Delhi: Segment Book Distributors,1989)

Haithcox, J. Patrick and D. L. Smith, American Colleges and the Study of Contemporary India, N. R. Inamdar, Chairman, Editorial Committee, in Felicitation to Professor V. M. Sirsikar, *Contemporary India: Socio-Economic and Political Processes*, (Poona: Continental Prakashan,1982)

Haynes, James, *A Lecturer's Tale*, (New York: Picador, 2002)

Johnson, Gordon, Chitpavan Brahmans and Politics in Western India in the Late Nineteenth and Early Twentieth Centuries. In Edmund Leach and S. N. Muherjee, eds., *Elites in South Asia* (Cambridge: Cambridge University Press, 1970, pp. 95-118.)

Joshi, A.C., Administrative Organization of Higher Education and Educational Planning, in G. S. Sharma, ed., *Educational Planning: Its Legal and*

Constitutional Implications in India, (Bombay: N. M. Tripathi Private Ltd, 1967) pp. 187-198.

Kamat, A.R., Politico-Economic Developments in Maharashtra: A Review of the Post-Independence Period, *Economic and Political Weekly*, part I, September 7, 1980b, pp. 1627-1630.

—— Politico-Economic Developments in Maharashtra: A Review of the Post-Independence Period. *Economic and Political Weekly*, part II, October 4, 1980b, pp. 1669-1678.

Kumar, Ravinder, *Western India in the Nineteenth Century: A study in the Social History of Maharashtra*, (London: Routledge & Kegan Pual, 1968)

Kurtz, Donald V., *Power and Paradigms: An Introduction to Political Anthropology*, (Boulder: Westview Press, 2001)

Lele, Jayant, *Elite Pluralism and Class Rule: Political Development in Mahahashtra, India*, (Toronto: University of Toronto Press, 1981)

—— One Party Domination in Maharashtra: Resistance and Change. In John R. Woods, ed., *State Politics in Contemporary India*, (Boulder: Westview Press, pp. 169-196.)

Marquit, Edwin, Philip Moran, and Willis H. Truit, eds. Dialectical Contradictions: Contemporary Marxist Discussions. *Studies in Marxism*, Vol. 10, (Minneapolis: Marxist Educational Press, 1982)

Murphy, Robert, *Dialectics of Social Life: Alarms and Excursions in Anthropological Theory*, (New York: Basic Books, 1971)

Nyop, Richard F. ed., *India: A Country Study. Foreign Area Studies*, (The American University: Washington, D.C., 1971)

O'Hanlon, Rosalind, 1985. *Caste, Conflict, and Ideology: Mahatma Jotirao Phule and Low Caste Protest in Nineteenth-Century Western India*, (Cambridge: Cambridge University Press, 1985)

Omvedt, Gail., *Cultural Revolt in a Colonial Society: The Non-Brahman Movement in Western India: 1873-1930*, (Bombay: Scientific Socialist Education Trust, 1976)

Rosenthal, Donald, *The Expansive Elites*, (Berkeley: University of California Press, 1977)

Sankalia, H.D., *Born for Archaeology: An Autobiography*, (New Delhi: B. R. Publishing Corporation, 1978)

Sirsikar, V.M., Linkage Politics in Maharashtra, in Iqbal Narain, ed., *State Politics in India*, (Meerut: Meenakashi, 1972)

—— *Politics of Modern Maharashtra*, (Hyderabad: Orient Longman, 1995)

Smiley, Jane, *Moo* (New York: Alfred A. Knopf, 1995)

Tickoo, Champa, *Indian Universities: A Historical, Contemporary Perspective*, (Bombay: Orient Longman, 1980)

Zelliot, Eleanor, Maratha: An Historical View of the Maharashtra Intellectual and Social Change, in Yogendra K. Malik, ed., *South Asian Intellectuals and Social Change: A Study of the Role of Vernacular-Speaking Intelligentsia*, (Columbia, Missouri: South Asian Books, 1982) pp. 18-88.

Index